The Resilient Self

Asian American Studies Today

This series publishes scholarship on cutting-edge themes and issues, including broadly based histories of both long-standing and more recent immigrant populations; focused investigations of ethnic enclaves and understudied subgroups; and examinations of relationships among various cultural, regional, and socioeconomic communities. Of particular interest are subject areas in need of further critical inquiry, including transnationalism, globalization, homeland polity, and other pertinent topics.

Series Editor: Huping Ling, Truman State University

The Resilient Self

~

Gender, Immigration, and Taiwanese Americans

CHIEN-JUH GU

Rutgers University Press

New Brunswick, Camden, and Newark, New Jersey, and London

Library of Congress Cataloging-in-Publication Data

Names: Gu, Chien-Juh, 1969– author.
Title: The resilient self : gender, immigration, and Taiwanese Americans /
Chien-Juh Gu.
Description: New Brunswick : Rutgers University Press, [2017] | Series: Asian
American studies today | Includes bibliographical references and index.
Identifiers: LCCN 2017011059 (print) | LCCN 2017026076 (ebook) |
ISBN 9780813586076 (E-pub) | ISBN 9780813586083 (Web PDF) |
ISBN 9780813586069 (cloth : alk. paper) | ISBN 9780813586052 (pbk. : alk. paper)
Subjects: LCSH: Taiwanese Americans—Social conditions. | Immigrant women—
United States—Social conditions. | Women—Taiwan—Identity. | Women—United
States—Identity. | Sex role—United States. | Resilience (Personality trait) |
United States—Emigration and immigration—Psychological aspects. |
Taiwan—Emigration and immigration—Psychological aspects.
Classification: LCC E184.T35 (ebook) | LCC E184.T35 G823 2017 (print) |
DDC 305.40951249—dc23
LC record available at https://lccn.loc.gov/2017011059

A British Cataloging-in-Publication record for this book is
available from the British Library.

∞ The paper used in this publication meets the requirements
of the American National Standard for Information Sciences—
Permanence of Paper for Printed Library Materials, ANSI Z39.48–1992.

www.rutgersuniversitypress.org

Manufactured in the United States of America

In memory of my parents and brother,
Chiu-Yueh Lin, Wen-Yen Gu, and Tom Gu

Contents

The Resilient Self

1
Introduction

It was a sunny afternoon in Chicago when I interviewed Jen, an immigrant woman from Taiwan who owns a computer company that handles millions of dollars in revenue each year. Confident, assertive, and passionate, Jen shared many of her experiences conducting business in mainstream U.S. society, including competing with White-owned companies and overcoming stereotypes of Asian women. I quietly admired the wisdom, strength, and sophisticated social skills revealed in her stories, but I was puzzled by her gloomy face when she spoke about her family life, especially her relationship with her in-laws. I will never forget the sadness, emptiness, and helplessness on her face as she said, "At work, I make all the decisions and I am in control, but at home, I have to be submissive. I feel so powerless and miserable. . . ."

The enormous contrast between Jen's sense of self in the work and family domains is not an isolated case. Since beginning my research on Taiwanese Americans a decade ago, I have heard similar stories from women repeatedly during interviews. Countless questions and puzzles occupied my mind during those sleepless nights while in the field collecting data. Why are these professional women so assertive at work but so passive at home? Why do they feel content with work regardless of their gender and race disadvantages, but remain powerless and suffer in their family lives where most immigrants' senses of security and satisfaction are rooted? Why do Taiwanese gender norms have such a persistent influence on their behaviors when interacting with in-laws even among those who have been acculturated into middle-class America for more than two decades?

Moreover, many professional women become housewives after immigration. For someone who is highly educated and who once had a prominent career, what does it mean to be a housewife in a foreign country? How do these women perceive themselves, their loss of career and an independent income, and their new status as a visible racial minority? What do immigrant women's experiences of adaptation and suffering tell us about the interplay of gender and immigration and its effects on individuals' lives? This book answers these questions.

International Migration as a Gendered Process and Experience

Immigration is fundamentally a gender issue.[1] Gendered labor markets and social networks contribute to varying immigration patterns, settlement processes, and adaptation experiences of both women and men.[2] International migration also often leads to the reconfiguration of gender relations and family power structures. For instance, immigrant women laborers have better employment opportunities than their male counterparts in many labor-intensive industries that desire female immigrant workers, such as the service, microelectronics, health care, and garment sectors.[3] Women's greater financial contributions to the family consequently enhance their status at home. Research has shown that Dominican immigrant women in New York's garment industry, Vietnamese immigrant women in Philadelphia, Mexican immigrant women in Iowa's meatpacking industry, and Korean immigrant women in urban Texas all gain greater bargaining power over their family budgets, and they are able to negotiate more sharing of household labor from their husbands because of the economic resources they brought to the family from employment.[4]

The increasing employment rate among Western women since the 1980s has also created the need for domestic labor. As a result, many working women hire female laborers from Latin America and Southeast Asia to serve as nannies or maids in their private homes.[5] Many of these domestic workers migrate alone, leaving their families behind. As a result, their husbands assume more childcare and household responsibilities, which reverses traditional gender roles. As the primary breadwinners, these immigrant maids and nannies contribute to their families' financial advancement, but they are also forced to entrust their children to others (i.e., husbands and extended families) while they care for other women's children and homes.

Industries that favor male laborers, such as construction and farming, attract many male immigrants who leave their families behind to seek employment opportunities overseas. For example, many Mexican immigrant men migrate alone to work as janitors, gardeners, and construction workers in the United States, primarily in California and Texas. Their connections with other Mexican men who have migrated north enable them to find employment through these male networks. Meanwhile, their wives stay in Mexico to care for their children and families. These women shoulder greater responsibilities around the house and act with autonomy and assertion. Over time, they also establish networks with Mexican immigrant women and are eventually able to mobilize their ethnic networks to persuade their husbands to relocate the entire family to the United States.[6]

Employment also reconfigures gender relations in middle-class immigrant families. In Korean, Chicano, Taiwanese, Indian, and Filipino immigrant families in which wives are professionals, husbands undertake more housework and childcare responsibilities compared to their lower-class counterparts. Scholars have provided several explanations for this phenomenon, including the high demands of these women's careers, the smaller earning gaps between the couple, women's abilities to negotiate more sharing, and husbands' added free time. These factors also result in more egalitarian gender ideologies among middle-class men compared to their laborer counterparts. Regardless, women continue to perform more housework duties compared to their husbands across ethnicity and country of origin.[7]

Immigrant entrepreneurs' lives are somewhat different. Many small immigrant businesses rely on unpaid wives and underpaid coethnic employees for their successes and profits.[8] In Pyong Gap Min's study of Korean immigrant businesses in New York City, wives play a critical role in operating family-owned stores. They work long hours and consider their labor an extension of their domestic obligations. However, their husbands are registered as the legal owners and dominate the decision-making power for both their stores and families. In immigrant-owned stores, the distinction between work and family is blurred as couples work side by side for long hours, and many do not hire additional workers. Tension sometimes arises in this work-is-also-family context.[9] Working and living in such an isolated environment also increases married women's financial and social dependence on their husbands.[10]

Miliann Kang's study of Korean-women-owned nail salons tells a different story. Nail salons give immigrant women a place to work separately from their husbands. They provide an independent source of income and greater economic opportunities for the family's upward mobility. Nevertheless, these salon owners often feel guilty about not devoting enough time to their roles as wives and mothers. They struggle to balance work, homemaking, and childcare responsibilities regardless of the autonomy and financial independence they gain through entrepreneurship.[11] In the United States, immigrant-women-owned businesses vary to a great extent, including law firms, architecture companies, travel agencies, childcare centers, and gift shops. Similar to the Korean immigrant women in Kang's study, these business owners also face common challenges in balancing work and family demands as well as in battling racial inequality and racism in the larger society.[12]

In all of these studies, scholars highlight the role of gender in constructing immigration patterns and settlement experiences. Analyses of gender are often situated in work-family contexts without explicitly stating the importance of gender-work-family connections.[13] More prevalently, many scholars examine immigrant women's and men's experiences in only the family or only the workplace. Few researchers have fully integrated gender and work-family contexts to examine the multifaceted connections of immigrant adaptation. In fact, immigration is not only a gendered process but also a work-family issue in its essence.[14] Work and family as major components of the social structure construct two interconnected institutions through which gender inequality is socially constituted.[15] Therefore, in immigration research, it is important to focus not only on gender but also on its association with the interplay of work, family, and other structural factors, an objective that this book aims to achieve.

Gendered Immigration in the Work-Family Context

Since the 1980s, a consistent theme has emerged from numerous studies of gender and immigration: immigrant women's labor force participation in the host society and their exposure to Western culture constitute two main factors that enhance their status and bargaining power at home.[16] In other words, scholars have suggested repeatedly that immigration somewhat emancipates women from patriarchal societies through their employment in the host society, although their gains and losses are uneven in different arenas.[17]

The case of Taiwanese American women has in many ways challenged this thesis and how we understand the effects of immigration and gender on women's family and work lives. For instance, Taiwanese immigrant husbands dominate decisions to settle their families in the United States, usually for their own job opportunities and career advancement. In the context in which husbands secure professional jobs in a Western society, married women are presented with limited choices. Out of concern for their family's well-being, many women give up high-paying, high-status jobs in Taiwan to accompany their husbands to the United States. Their motives for settlement are overwhelmingly driven by social and family factors, including their children's education, living environment, and factors other than their own job opportunities.[18]

Migrating as dependents, many professional women retreat from prominent careers to become homemakers. Their employment is restricted not only by their visa status but also by their *cumulative disadvantage*, in Bandana Purkayastha's term.[19] Unable to work outside the home, immigrant housewives' sense of self-worth increasingly relies on their children's achievements, rather than their own; they are overwhelmed by the overload of domestic work, but consider housework their sole responsibility. In other words, immigration ties Taiwanese women closer to the domestic sphere and intensifies the work-family division, a phenomenon I call *housewifelization* (see chapter 3). Although many women manage to enter the U.S. labor force later, most choose fields that differ from their original training for practical reasons. The meaning of work changes for them, and having a career is no longer their ambition. The new meaning of employment also partly influences how professional women handle mistreatment and racial inequality in the workplace (see chapter 6).

Previous studies have also considered immigrant women's exposure to Western culture as a main factor that awakens their egalitarian desire to negotiate an equal share of housework with their husbands, even though such progressive behavior does not translate to their compliance in the workplace. Quite differently, most Taiwanese women in my study use practical reasoning when explaining their gender division of work at home (see chapter 4). For example, "Housewives are home all day long, so they should assume all housework" and "who is better at math should be in charge of family finances" are common rationalizations when subjects explained who did what around the house. In contrast, their cultural consciousness, whether Taiwanese/Asian or American/Western, is more evident in dealing with in-law (see chapter 5) and interracial relations (see chapter 6).

In other words, the interplay of immigration and gender, its interactive effects with work and family structures, and the consequent influences in individuals' lives are much more complicated than what the existing literature of gender and immigration suggests. In this book, I provide a more complex picture of the multifaceted connections of immigration, gender, work, family, race and ethnicity, citizenship, and culture in women's adaptation processes. I demonstrate how these intertwined structures reshape women's senses of self, construct the meanings they give to their paid and unpaid work, and affect how they interpret their behaviors in different relational contexts.

Women's Standpoint and Intersectionality

Women's experiences of immigration were absent in sociology for most of the twentieth century, as it was not until the mid-1980s that scholars began to include women in their studies.[20] The long absence of women's stories in immigration research not only reflects a gender-blind perspective but also an unbalanced source of knowledge production.

As feminist standpoint theory argues, women's unique standpoints in society offer a privileged vantage point on male supremacy. As Nancy Hartsock explains, the social structures that organize, shape, limit, and penetrate the everyday world vary for people in different social locations and shape different experiences of life. However, women's voices are often suppressed in both society and social sciences. She argues that women's experiences allow scholars to go beneath the surface of the social world and reveal concealed social relations. Thus, women's perspectives and experiences should be central to knowledge, culture, and politics.[21]

Dorothy Smith followed this intellectual tradition and developed a sociological method from the standpoint of women. Criticizing how women's lives are absent from the domain of sociology, she argues that sociology must be rooted in the life world of women's standpoints, material realities, and local experiences that are always situated, relational, and engaged.[22] Sandra Harding also contends that research should begin with women's lives because it leads to socially constructed claims that are less false, less distorted, and less partial than those of men's lives.[23] Noting the importance of women's voices, standpoint theorists have clarified that women do not occupy a single standpoint. Rather, women's life experiences are diverse because of their different social locations that are shaped not only by gender but also by other social variables such as race, social class, and sexuality.

Patricia Hill Collins articulates a Black feminist standpoint that underlines the common experiences of Black women as differing from those of Whites and that recognizes the differences among Black women themselves.[24] Collins's work has greatly influenced the development of the concept of *intersectionality* in feminist thought since the 1990s. Central to contemporary gender scholarship, intersectionality examines the interlocking inequalities created by gender, race, class, sexuality, and other social positions and the multilayered oppression that individuals experience through power relations in varied ways and on different levels (macro, meso, and micro) of social life.[25]

Highlighting the heterogeneity of women's experiences, however, does not mean that endless segmented stories exist in research. Susan Hekman explains that knowledge is situated, located, and shaped by individual perspectives. By making persuasive arguments based on subjects' accounts of the world, standpoint theorists can achieve feminist objectivity and avoid absolute relativism.[26] Donna Haraway further elaborates that feminist models of scientific knowledge, what she calls *rational knowledge* or *situated knowledge*, should be a power-sensitive conversation that provides a common ground for dialog, rationality, and objectivity. In her viewpoint, the production of situated knowledge is, by its nature, a process of ongoing critical interpretations of subjects' accounts of their situated life worlds. Although subjects are the object of knowledge, they must be considered as agents.[27]

Feminist standpoint theory frames both the epistemology and analytical approach of this study. I ground my research on women's standpoints and use subjects' narratives as the main source of data to illuminate their experiences and perspectives from their social locations (being female, middle class, Asian, Taiwanese, and foreign-born Americans). This approach treats subjects as agents of knowledge, not simply as recipients of social forces. I highlight major patterns that emerged from their life stories and note variations to show heterogeneity and avoid reductionism. I pay close attention to power dynamics and subjectivities in each relational context to uncover inequality and dialectical relations between individuals and social structure.

Social Structure, Culture, and Self

Alienation and marginality have constituted the main themes of classic studies on immigration. Almost a century ago, William Thomas and Florian Znaniecki's book, *The Polish Peasant in Europe and America*, documented the lives of Polish peasant immigrants in Europe and the United States. They examined the relations between individuals and their surrounding societies and explored how families and ethnic communities adapted to changes in the process of immigration. They discussed the role of immigrants' cultures of origin in affecting both the adjustment and maladjustment of their lives in the receiving society. They also documented the struggle for self-esteem among young male immigrants.[28]

In *The Uprooted*, Oscar Handlin documented the fears, hopes, and expectations that European immigrants experienced in their American lives.[29] In *The Marginal Man*, Everett Stonequist discussed the double-edged marginality of immigrants' social locations.[30] Both books uncover the emotions and feelings of immigrants, as well as the potential risks of immigration to individuals' well-being. They speak to the fundamental human needs for belongingness and the often unspoken difficulties and pain of being immigrants.

These classic studies demonstrate that immigration is not just patterns of human movement and resettlement. Rather, individuals' hearts and souls experience ups and downs in their adaptation processes as they sometimes struggle to find meaning and niches for themselves in the new land. As Steve Gold contends, immigration is one of the most drastic actions that people can take in their lifetimes because it involves taking social, financial, cultural, and psychological risks.[31] Therefore, individuals' subjective understandings and lived experiences of immigration provide an important topic for sociological research.

In fact, the focus of these classic studies—the relation between individuals and their surrounding societal contexts—has been a central theme in sociology and social psychology since the publication of George H. Mead's *Mind, Self, & Society*.[32] However, contemporary studies of gender and immigration have rarely addressed the deepest human yearning and questioning in the process of settlement: Who am I? Am I still the person I was before immigration? What has changed about me and what has not as a result of immigration? What caused these changes and how? Where is my place in the new land? How should I behave as an immigrant? This book explores this classic theme by bringing the self into the study of gender and immigration.

Sociologically speaking, the self differs from identity. While identity is associated with social positions, roles, or group memberships (e.g., gender, race, nurse), the self refers to a broader understanding of the individual as a whole. Sheldon Stryker explains that the self is organized into multiple parts (identities), each of which is tied to aspects of the social structure.[33] Sociologists prioritize the role of social forces in conceptualizing the self, and emphasize the agency through which social actors define selfhood and negotiate the meaning of their actions. Anthony Giddens uses the term *reflexivity* to describe a self-defining process in which individuals reflect upon both social and psychological information about possible life trajectories. For Giddens, individuals' sense-making processes are rich, profound, and sophisticated social practices, especially when they involve uncertainty and anxiety. Giddens uses marriage to exemplify how divorce, the dissolution of marriage, can call an individual into an emotional engagement with the self as one questions and rebuilds him or herself in facing the pain and change of life.[34] Following Giddens, the changes that immigration brings to life can also generate such a sense-making, self-searching process as international migration involves uncertainty, risks, losses, struggles, and tremendous adaptation.

Sociological theories of the self lie at the heart of social psychology, especially in the work of Mead and Erving Goffman. According to Mead, the self is not initially in an individual, but arises in the process of social experience and activity. It evolves in an individual as a result of his or her relations to the process as a whole and to other individuals within that process. People develop minds through role taking or how they think others perceive them. In other words, individuals' choices of behavior are always linked to social structures and constraints. The meaning they give to their choices and behaviors is also socially situated and emerges in social interactions. From this symbolic interactionist viewpoint, people do not simply do what they do. Rather, individuals make choices based on how they understand their roles, contexts, and interactions with others. Mead argues that language is central to the constitution of the self. Individuals' subjective interpretations and descriptions of their lived experiences provide important materials to understand the evolution of the self and its dialectical connections to the social world. In this study, I analyze subjects' narratives of their life histories and immigration experiences to unlock the intertwined connections of immigration, gender, work, family, culture, race and ethnicity, citizenship, and the self in the lives of middle-class Taiwanese American women.

In *The Presentation of Self in Everyday Life*, Goffman explains how the self consists of the multiplicity of roles performed in different situated contexts.[35] Following this viewpoint, immigrants' daily decisions are conditioned by the social, economic, and cultural contexts of the host society. In the process of acculturation and adaptation, immigrants develop their minds by taking on the roles of foreign-born individuals in the United States, in general, and in various social institutions, in particular (e.g., workplace and family). Their interactions with others in different social settings also shape their perspectives and behaviors, as well as the meanings and interpretations they give to their choices and behaviors. In this book, I examine four situated contexts: housewives' lives in early family settlement years (chapter 3), spousal relations in the family (chapter 4), in-law relations in three-generation households (chapter 5), and workplace and community experiences (chapter 6). These contexts represent different sites of analysis, where the multifaceted connections of gender, work, family, immigration, culture, race and ethnicity, citizenship, and the self are manifested in varied ways. Together, they reveal the complex construction of the self and its profound and compound relevance to the social world.

Description of the Research

This book is mainly based on life-history interviews with forty-five middle-class Taiwanese immigrant women, supplemented by ethnographic observations over seven years (2007–2014) and findings from my previous project on Taiwanese Americans (fifty-four in-depth interviews with both men and women; both first- and second-generation immigrants).[36] I conducted the study in urban Midwest regions of the Chicago metropolitan area and in southwest Michigan. All names used in this book are pseudonyms.

In 2007, when I took a faculty position at Western Michigan University, in Kalamazoo, which is located in southwest Michigan, about 150 miles from Chicago, I began to conduct ethnographic observations in the local ethnic-Chinese immigrant community that, at the time, composed of approximately 120 households, among which fifteen were Taiwanese. I joined a Chinese immigrant organization in this area (which had about four hundred members) and regularly attended formal and informal social gatherings, during which I observed social interactions and gender relations in the community. I worked as the treasurer and a substitute teacher at a weekend Chinese school run by Taiwanese immigrant housewives. I also met with ethnic-Chinese immigrant women (usually fifteen to twenty-five women, mostly housewives) for lunch monthly. I took field notes to document my observations and took pictures at these events. My participation in these social groups not only provided me with accessible networks to approach potential housewife interviewees, it also helped me gain firsthand experience and in-depth understanding of the social lives of local ethnic-Chinese immigrants, especially the Taiwanese. Numerous casual conversations in the field supplemented my interview data with important information.

From 2008 to 2011, I frequently traveled to Chicago to interview professional Taiwanese immigrant women, who worked in a range of fields, including computer science, accounting, pharmaceuticals, and academia. I adopted the life history approach to examine major changes in these women's self-concepts, gender relations, and racialized experiences in the process of settlement.[37] Using a semistructured interview schedule, I conducted life-history interviews with thirty-three women that ranged from three to twelve hours over up to four sessions with each subject. Two interviews were conducted in California during my trips to conferences because these subjects heard about my research from their friends in Chicago and were eager to tell me their life stories.

From 2011 to 2014, I conducted life-history interviews with twelve middle-class Taiwanese immigrant housewives, among whom nine were in southwest Michigan and three were in Chicago. Using a semistructured interview schedule similar to that used to interview professional subjects, I explored major changes in immigrant women's self-concepts and gender relations over time. While I discussed work relations and racial inequality in the workplace with professionals, I asked housewives questions about their racialized experiences in the larger U.S. society, such as at their children's schools, in their neighborhoods, and in their daily lives. Although unemployed, these homemakers were highly educated and highly skilled: four held advanced U.S. degrees (one PhD and three master's degrees), five held bachelor's degrees from Taiwan, and three had acquired professional diplomas in Taiwan (fifteen years of formal education). Their husbands were all professionals who worked in either large corporations or academic settings. My interviews with housewives ranged from two to four hours.

In summary, the forty-five subjects include thirty-three professionals and twelve housewives ranging in age from thirty to sixty-two (see appendix for subjects' demographic information). They immigrated to the United States between 1968 and 2006. Except for one permanent resident, all subjects had acquired citizenship at the time of the interviews. My interviews were conducted in Chinese or Taiwanese, and all were recorded and transcribed verbatim. Using the life history approach, my questions typically started by inquiring about their lives in Taiwan (childhood, schooling years, family relations, employment, career goals, and so forth), why they decided to move to the United States, and how they adjusted to their new lives in the United States. Self-concepts, gender relations, and racial relations were the main foci in my interviews. The inductive approach suggested by grounded theory was used to analyze major patterns that emerged from the interviews.[38]

Objective and Overview of the Book

The objective of this book is twofold. First, I use women's narratives of their life histories as the main source of data to recount the subjective experiences of immigration over time and in different relational contexts. Treating subjects as agents of knowledge, I chronicle how the women understand themselves in relation to others and their surrounding environments. Second, through subjects' stories, I seek to uncover how the multilayered connections of gender, immigration, work, family, race and ethnicity, citizenship, and culture shape these women's lived experiences. Rather than giving primacy to any single social variable, I unfold the uneven effects of the intertwined structural factors on the self in various contexts; this shows not only the complexity of immigrant lives but also the dialectical relations between individuals and social structure.

This book is composed of seven chapters. This chapter includes an introduction to the purpose, epistemology, objective, and organization of the book. The chapter also includes a review of the literature of gender and immigration and the importance and contributions of this study. Also described are the research methods and subjects' characteristics. Chapter 2 provides a description of the history, migration patterns, and socioeconomic characteristics of the Taiwanese in the United States. The chapter also includes an introduction to Taiwanese cultural traditions, especially Confucian cultural values of gender, family, work ethics, and relational harmony. I use the term *pan-Confucian culture* to describe the broad cultural atmosphere in Asian and Asian American communities under the influence of Confucianism; however, I urge caution about the danger of homogenizing Asian Americans, and instead highlight their heterogeneity. I compare different middle-class Asian immigrant women to discuss how intersectional structural factors, especially ethnicity, shape individuals' perceptions, attitudes, behaviors, and social practices.

Chapters 3 through 6 include the main empirical findings of this study. Chapter 3 includes documentation of subjects' struggles in questioning and searching for self during the early years of their family settlement. I coin the term *housewifelization* to describe how married women are tied more closely to the domestic sphere as a result of gendered immigration. Examining subjects' work trajectories over time, I discuss the women's lost selves, misemployment, meaning of work, nostalgia, and imagined selves as they navigate their immigrant lives in the new land.

Chapters 4 and 5 document two relational contexts in Taiwanese immigrant households: spousal and in-law relations. In chapter 4, I analyze subjects' rationalizations concerning their division of domestic labor and decision-making power over family finances to discuss gender ideologies, gender practices, and gender strategies among Taiwanese couples. I discuss the women's domestic and capable selves, as revealed in their interpretations of gender relations. In chapter 5, I describe in-law dynamics within three-generation households to illustrate the enormous cultural constraints of Confucian womanhood on subjects' lives. I also discuss the women's silenced selves in their cultural compliance, its consequent distress, the roles of their significant others (both their husbands and mothers), and coethnics' attitudes about gender norms in the Taiwanese community.

Chapter 6 chronicles women's racialized experiences in the United States. This chapter includes stories of subjects' encounters with racial prejudice and mistreatment in the workplace, at grocery stores, at their children's schools, and in their neighborhoods.

I illustrate how subjects' sense of their American selves in inter-racial interactions construct the meaning of these encounters and affect how they negotiate better treatment and individual rights. Finally, chapter 7 includes a summary of the findings of the study and theoretical implications. I explain how the findings illumi-nate the multifaceted connections of gender, immigration, work, family, culture, race and ethnicity, citizenship, and the self as they are manifested in varied ways during the process of adaptation and in the women's lived experiences.

2

Immigration, Culture, Gender, and the Self

How do I see myself? I'm Taiwanese American, but it's not 50 [percent Taiwanese] and 50 [percent American]. It's more like 75 percent [Taiwanese] and 55 percent [American]; sometimes 60 [percent Taiwanese] and 80 [percent American], when I am thinking about how to behave and which cultural norm I should follow. It really depends on the situation.
—Cindy, 40, PhD, scientist

Who are Taiwanese Americans? Given the scarce research on Taiwanese Americans, scholarly understanding of this ethnic group remains limited. Among the few studies about Taiwanese immigrants, Hsiang-Shui Chen's *Chinatown No More* is the first book to clarify the different social, economic, and cultural characteristics of the Taiwanese and the Chinese. Analyzing one hundred households of Taiwanese immigrants in Flushing, New York, Chen reports that most Taiwanese immigrants have high incomes, advanced education, professional jobs, and live in suburbs that are typically White majority areas. This portrait is evidently distinctive from the Chinese laborers and ethnic enclaves in Chinatown.[1]

In her study of Little Taipei (Monterey Park) in Los Angeles, Yen-Fen Tseng reports that Taiwanese immigrant entrepreneurship takes a completely different path from the traditional development of the ethnic economy, especially that of Chinatown. The Taiwanese possess better financial resources than most immigrants. Their businesses quickly develop beyond the original concentration and spread throughout the geographical area. Their economic impact on the larger society and social integration with the majority culture also differs from many other immigrant enterprises.[2] Both Chen's and Tseng's studies provide important empirical analyses about Taiwanese immigrants and highlight their significant differences from the Chinese. Since the publication of these works, scholars no longer mistake the Taiwanese for the Chinese.

In *Taiwanese Americans*, historian Franklin Ng names the Taiwanese as one of the newest American ethnic groups. He thoroughly introduces Taiwanese Americans' origins, immigration history, socioeconomic-political characteristics, and cultural traditions.[3] In my study conducted in Chicago, *Mental Health among Taiwanese Americans*, I document various sources of distress that Taiwanese American men and women encounter in the work and family domains. I examine gender differences in reaction to stressful situations and discuss how individuals negotiate agency in various social contexts.[4] In *Getting Saved in America*, Carolyn Chen discusses how two religions, Christianity and Buddhism, shape the Taiwanese experience of immigration. She argues that Taiwanese immigrants become American by becoming religious and they become religious by becoming American. In other words, religion plays a key role in the Taiwanese immigrant acculturation process.[5]

All of these studies have enhanced scholarly understanding of Taiwanese Americans. Meanwhile, several celebrities and public figures have also increased the visibility of this small ethnic group in U.S. society, including the award-winning film director Ang Lee, National Basketball Association player Jeremy Lin, fashion designer Jason Wu, journalist and anchor Connie Chung, AIDS researcher David Ho, and former U.S. secretary of labor and now secretary of transportation Elaine Chao. A recent ABC drama, *Fresh Off the Boat*, features a Taiwanese immigrant family in Orlando, Florida. Its popularity has enhanced public understanding of Taiwanese immigrants, although the show also reinforces many Asian stereotypes.[6]

In this chapter, I introduce the history and patterns of Taiwanese immigration in the United States. I also provide an overview of the socioeconomic characteristics of Taiwanese immigrants. Following this introduction, I explain major cultural values in the Taiwanese tradition, including gender-role expectations, family structure and practices, work ethics, and relational harmony. Like other Asian and Asian American communities, Taiwanese immigrants' beliefs and behaviors are greatly influenced by Confucianism. However, it does not mean that all Asians exhibit the same set of cultural characteristics. I use the term *pan-Confucian culture* to describe the general cultural outlook and discuss variations among Asian immigrants. Next, I discuss the complex interconnections of immigration, culture, gender, and the self.

Taiwanese Immigrants in the United States

Taiwan is an island located ninety-six miles east of the southern China coast. Roughly the size of Maryland, it had a population of 23.5 million in 2015. Because of its geographic proximity, Chinese immigration to Taiwan began as early as the sixteenth century, building close historical and cultural ties between China and Taiwan. When the Kuomintang (KMT) government lost the civil war to the Chinese Communist Party in 1949, its leader and supporters retreated to Taiwan.[7] Therefore, immigrants from Taiwan to the United States also include those who moved from China to Taiwan prior to their resettlement to U.S. society. This group tends to identify with China and consider themselves Chinese immigrants or Chinese Americans.

Taiwanese immigration to the United States began in the 1960s. In 2010, 358,460 Taiwan-born individuals were living in the United States, and Taiwanese immigrants were much more likely to be naturalized than the foreign born overall. However, because not all Taiwan-born individuals identified themselves as Taiwanese or had acquired citizenship, only 196,691 were listed as Taiwanese Americans in the 2010 Census.[8] In spite of their short history and presence in U.S. society, the Taiwan-born population increased more than fourfold, from 81,300 in 1980 to 358,460 in 2010, with a growth rate of 67.6 percent from 2000 (199,192) to 2010.[9] The size of this population is comparable to that of recent Italian and Brazilian immigrants.

Immigrants from Taiwan, China, and Hong Kong comprise the three major ethnic Chinese American groups.[10] Although sharing the Confucian tradition, these three groups have distinct historical, economic, social, and political backgrounds that characterize their life experiences, worldviews, and immigration-related issues such as migration motives, abilities to migrate, policies under which they entered the United States, and resources they bring with them.[11] Therefore, it is important to recognize the heterogeneity among ethnic-Chinese groups and the distinctiveness of Taiwanese immigrants in the United States.

In contrast to Chinese immigrants, who have an over 150-year-long history in the United States, Taiwanese living in the United States are primarily post-1965 immigrants. Unlike Chinese immigrants, many of whom are laborers residing in ethnic enclaves, such as Chinatown, Taiwanese immigrants are scattered throughout suburban White areas, and the majority are professionals. No particular landscape or ethnic enclave marks this community.[12] About half of Taiwanese immigrants live in California; the San Jose-Sunnyvale-Santa Clara area has the highest population of Taiwanese immigrants. Several metropolitan areas also attract large numbers of Taiwanese immigrants, such as Los Angeles and San Francisco, California; Flushing and Queens, New York; Seattle, Washington; Houston, Texas; and Chicago, Illinois.[13]

Most Taiwanese immigrants initially came to the United States in pursuit of higher education, especially in scientific fields. Because the 1965 Immigration Act created a new set of preference categories that prioritized two groups—those who came for family reunification and those with professional skills—many U.S.-trained Taiwanese students were able to apply for permanent residency for themselves and their families after graduation. According to Shirley Chang, from the 1960s to the 1980s, more than

80 percent of Taiwanese students who completed their graduate studies in the United States did not return to Taiwan.[14] Therefore, the majority of Taiwanese immigrants are U.S.-trained professionals. This trend has continued, although with some fluctuations over time. *Immigration through education* remains the major pattern of Taiwanese immigration to the United States. Unlike many other professional immigrant groups and their lower-class counterparts who are determined to settle in the United States to pursue better economic opportunities, most middle-class Taiwanese immigrants consider return to always be an option.[15]

In *Immigrant America*, Alejandra Portes and Rubén Rumbaut list the Taiwanese as one of the country's major brain drain groups.[16] Indeed, Taiwanese Americans are the most educated ethnic group in the United States. In 2010, 73.7 percent held bachelor degrees or higher, which was significantly higher than the American average (17.6 percent). Almost two-thirds of employed adult Taiwanese immigrants worked as professionals and managers.[17] Most notably, both Taiwanese immigrant men and women present a high-education, high-income professional profile. In 1999, employed Taiwanese immigrant men earned an average annual income of $60,367, surpassing that of foreign-born men by nearly $20,000. Employed Taiwanese women earned $40,276 in the same year, about $10,000 more than the average earnings for all foreign-born women in the United States. Both men's and women's income levels were also significantly higher compared to their Asian counterparts from India, China, Korea, and Japan. Further, the majority of Taiwanese Americans were naturalized through employment-based routes. This population also had a higher rate of homeownership and lower poverty rate than U.S. natives and all immigrants.[18]

Early Taiwanese immigrants' homogeneity began to change in the 1980s, making the second wave of Taiwanese immigration more diverse.[19] In 1981, Congress set an annual quota of 20,000 Taiwanese immigrants that took effect in 1982. Although the inflow of college students from Taiwan continued, newcomers in the mid- and late 1980s included many businesspeople and working-class families. These new immigrants had not studied in the United States and often lacked proficiency in English. In contrast to their professional counterparts who lived in the suburbs, they tended to reside in ethnic enclaves such as Flushing and Queens, New York, and Monterey Park, California.[20] The diversity of Taiwanese immigrants has increased ever since.

Over the past two decades, a considerable proportion of Taiwanese immigrants have been transnational families, especially in California. Typically, the mother and children migrate to the United States, while the father remains in Taiwan to work. These fathers usually have prestigious jobs in Taiwan and comfortably occupy the middle or upper-middle classes. The primary goal for Taiwanese transnational families is for their children to receive a better education, which is an immigration motive that significantly differs from transnational laborers who migrate to enhance their families' economic conditions. In some cases, school-age Taiwanese children or youths live with relatives who are immigrants, while their parents remain in Taiwan.[21]

The greater Chicago area, where my research is largely based, is an important geographic site because more than 80 percent of Taiwanese immigrants in the Midwest reside in this region. The Taiwanese population is among the top five fastest growing ethnic groups in the Chicago metropolitan area (it grew 61 percent from 2000 to 2010). Most notably, the Taiwanese have the highest educational attainment among all ethnic groups in the area. In fact, 97 percent of the Taiwanese twenty-five years and older have a high school degree or higher, and 84 percent hold bachelor's degrees or higher. While their highest educational level is congruent with the educational achievement of Taiwanese nationally, these numbers are significantly higher than those in the national data (73.7 percent of Taiwanese in the United States hold a BA or higher). Moreover, 66 percent of the Taiwanese in Chicago own their homes, slightly higher than the rate of all residents in the same area (65 percent). They also have the second lowest rate of low-income population (15 percent), only slightly higher than the Filipinos (14 percent). However, a large portion of the low-income

Taiwanese live in poverty (10 percent), much higher than the poverty rate for Filipinos (5 percent).[22] These data suggest that while Chicago has mostly typical middle-class Taiwanese, a significant portion of poor Taiwanese warrants future research to better understand the contrast between the two subgroups.

Confucian Cultural Values in the Taiwanese Tradition

Confucianism profoundly shapes Taiwanese culture. Historically, Confucian ideology has long been taught and emphasized in Taiwanese schools. The Taiwanese government mandated that Confucianism be incorporated into formal education and standardized textbooks. It is not only part of the school curriculum but also a moral foundation for behavior and social order. Children begin to learn Confucian cultural values at a young age both at school and in the family. Before 2001, Confucianism was a formal academic subject in both middle and elementary schools that students had to study and be tested on, just like math and science.[23] Even after the educational reform in 2001 that removed this subject from the school curriculum, emphasis on Confucian ethics and morality has continued in both informal education and the family.[24] As a fundamental force of socialization, Confucianism greatly shapes social norms, moral values, and appropriate behavior in Taiwan. It also affects the formulation of laws and public policies on the island.

Below, I explain two aspects of Confucian culture that are relevant to this study: (1) gender and family norms and (2) work ethics and the value of relational harmony. These cultural values will help illuminate some of the perceptions and behaviors narrated in this book.

GENDER AND FAMILY NORMS

According to Confucian morality, men's social status is higher than that of women's. The cultural aphorism that "men are superior; women subordinate" (*nan zhun nu bei*) highlights the traditional Taiwanese worldview of gender: men are to exercise ruling power in both public and private arenas, while women are to be obedient, modest, and quiet. In Confucianism, a virtuous woman is the one with no ability and no ambition; a married woman should obey her husband and should always follow her husband wherever he is, no matter what kind of person he is or what job he does.[25] In contemporary Taiwan, improvements in women's education and social status, growth in women's participation in the labor market, and a wide diffusion of Western culture and feminist thought have promoted egalitarian ideologies and practices among men and women. Nevertheless, scholars have observed that gender relations on the island remain grounded in traditional cultural norms.[26]

The family is the foundation of ethnic-Chinese societies, including Taiwan. Many core Confucian values are highlighted in Taiwanese family practices. For instance, husbands are considered the head of the household, and they are entrusted with decision making for the family. Wives are responsible for providing stable, caring home environments for their husbands and the next generation. According to Confucianism, married women's duties are to support their husbands and raise their children (*xiang fu jiao zi*). In public discourse and the media, married women are often praised when they prioritize their husbands' success and family well-being over their own careers or personal needs. Wives' devotion, especially when it involves sacrifices, is considered essential for family prosperity as it signifies the central value of Confucian womanhood. The statement, "There is always a good woman behind a successful man," is often expressed in the media to attribute a man's achievements to his supportive wife who is typically portrayed as someone who is dutiful, quiet, out of the spotlight, often without a career of her own, and shoulders all household and childraising responsibilities. In some cases, tolerating their husbands' affairs is also considered a virtue of married women.

Filial piety is another important family value in Taiwan. Confucian principles of filial piety demand children's absolute obedience and complete devotion to parents, obligating children to repay parents by caring for them and providing financial support. The twenty-four stories of filial piety are included in textbooks and taught in elementary schools. For example, one of these stories depicts a child who goes shirtless at night to attract mosquitos so his parents can have a good night sleep without getting mosquito bites. This story conveys the message that children ought to prioritize their parents' well-being over their own, even when it involves sacrifices. Confucian teaching also instills the concept that parents are always right, so the cause of any conflict between the two generations must be the result of the children's inappropriate attitudes and behaviors. Thus, it is the children's responsibility to seek reconciliation by apology and self-condemnation when their parents are unhappy.[27]

Confucian cultural values of filial piety are encouraged and implemented in Taiwanese social life. For instance, the Taiwanese government not only advocates three-generation cohabitation by providing tax exemptions and subsidizes, it also criminalizes the behavior of abandoning parents. According to Taiwan's Criminal Code (Articles 294 and 295), the sentence for a person who abandons his or her linear blood relative ranges from six months to eight years.[28] Moreover, the mass media reinforces the value of filial piety by portraying happy three-generation households in Taiwan in contrast to the lonely, sad, and abandoned elderly in Western societies.[29] In other words, three-generation households are perceived as more than just a social norm; they are a highly valued human virtue rooted in Confucianism.

Following the morality of filial piety, three-generation cohabitation (patrilocal) is highly valued because it reflects this Confucian teaching. The three Ps—patriarchal, patrilocal, and patrilineal—mark the Taiwanese family structure.[30] Extended families centered on patrilineal kinship are the primary circle of social relations. Veneration of age demands similar obedience, as it requires the younger generation to honor their elders with deference, respect, and compliance.[31] In patrilocal households, the daughter-in-law occupies the lowest status, even lower than that of her sons. A daughter-in-law is expected to live with and serve her parents-in-law, an act that is strongly tied to the ideal of Confucian womanhood.[32]

Culturally, the mother-in-law is given the power to socialize the daughter-in-law into her proper role in the patrilocal household, through which the mother-in-law gains power over the younger woman while also helping sustain patriarchy. Feminist scholars have criticized the ideology of three-generation cohabitation as gender-blind because it is implemented at the price of immeasurable repression of daughters-in-law who serve and subordinate themselves to sustain the patriarchal system.[33] As Judith Stacey contends, the mother-in-law is "patriarchy's female deputy" in the Chinese family.[34] In this culture, a mother-in-law is entitled to demand, discipline, and even physically punish her daughter-in-law, and a daughter-in-law's failure to fulfill her expected gender role (i.e., obeying her mother-in-law) incurs social stigma. As a result, mistreatment is not uncommon, and a daughter-in-law's discontentment is fairly prevalent in Taiwanese society. Given its theatrical and tragic nature, the mother-in-law/daughter-in-law dynamic has also been the topic of numerous TV dramas on the island.

WORK ETHICS AND THE VALUE OF RELATIONAL HARMONY

Confucian work ethics place a high value on hard work, humbleness, and relational harmony. Several cultural aphorisms derived from stories of famous intellectuals in ancient China illustrate some of these cultural values: "Diligence is the means by which one makes up for one's dullness" (*qin neng bu zhou*); "A pestle can be ground into a needle and true knowledge comes from perseverance"; and "With determination and perseverance, one can overcome any obstacle." In other words, diligence and perseverance are considered important virtues and keys to success.

In *Confucius: The Analects*, Tzu-kung says, "The Master gets it through being cordial, well-behaved, respectful, frugal, and deferential."[35] This statement reveals the emphasis on qualities of introversion within Confucian teaching. Confucianism not only highly values humility but also condemns crafty language in self-expression. Confucius always teaches students: "It is rare, indeed, for a man with cunning words and an ingratiating countenance to be benevolent."[36] Several old sayings in Taiwanese society reinforce these Confucian values. For example, the cultural aphorisms, "Silence is gold" and "Empty vessels make the most sound," both applaud quietness and condemn self-promotion.[37] This culture shapes the belief that a person who possesses great abilities is usually discreet and humble; in contrast, when someone has to tell others how good he or she is, it reflects this person's superficiality and ignorance. Again, Confucian culture cultivates restrained temperament.

Harmony (*he*) is a central theme of Confucianism, a concept that penetrates all dimensions of Confucian discourse. It is not only a principle for human existence that seeks the moral correspondence between humans and the Way of Heaven; it also provides practical means to solve social conflicts and maintain social order. The Confucian Way of Harmony indicates the need to overcome tension in social relations. Confucian teaching calls for the cultivation of one's virtues when conflict arises from the relation between the self and others. By cultivating one's character, a person can extend his or her virtue to others. Thus, accomplishing relational harmony requires individuals to look beyond their personal desires and have others' interests in mind.[38] In other words, Confucian culture perceives self-centeredness as a barrier to harmonious relationships with others. Thus, confrontation is discouraged, as it would disturb relational harmony.

In summary, Confucianism nurtures a culture that values social order, hierarchical structures and statues (centered on gender, generation, and age), relational harmony, humility, quietness, filial piety, and moral virtues. Confucian ideology shapes many Asian and Asian American cultures; however, its actual effects are by no means homogeneous. Next, I discuss the heterogeneous cultural representations shaped by Confucian influence.

Pan-Confucian Culture and Its Heterogeneity: Ethnicity, Family, Social Class, and Women's Choices

Confucianism is a cultural, moral, and ideological system that has produced profound influences on Asian and Asian American societies—what I call a *pan-Confucian culture*. Similar to how the cultural logic of capitalism affects Western societies, Confucianism largely shapes Asian cultures. Nevertheless, this does not mean that a universal cultural representation exists under the Confucian influence. It would also be problematic to use Confucianism unquestionably to explain everything in Asia or Asian America. In fact, variations exist among different Asian and Asian American cultures. Even within an ethnic Asian group, the impact of Confucianism on individuals' values and behaviors is rarely identical or consistent.

In real life, how an individual uses cultural resources to guide behavior or interpret the meaning of a social interaction depends on various factors, such as the setting, the nature of the relation, structural positions of all social actors involved (i.e., gender, race, class, sexuality, nationality), and even emotions and personalities. As a cultural system, Confucianism is not a list of fixed characteristics. In a global era in which culture penetrates national borders, it is impossible to locate where the influence of one culture ends and the other begins.

For instance, Taiwanese immigrants in the United States are influenced by both Confucian and American cultures. Meanwhile, they form a distinct Taiwanese American culture as they adapt to the host society over time (so-called *creolization*). Their cultural values are also shaped by individual positions (such as gender, sexuality, and social class) and can change in different contexts and time periods. Therefore, Taiwanese American culture is not a fifty–fifty mix of two cultures; neither is it the sum of Confucian and American cultures. Using Cindy's words when describing her dual culture: "It's more like 75 percent [Taiwanese] and 55 percent [American]; sometimes 60 [percent Taiwanese] and 80 [percent American] when I am thinking about how to behave and which cultural norm I should follow. It really depends on the situation."

Ann Swidler's concept of a *cultural toolkit* is useful to understand the contextual, fluid, and complex nature of culture.[39] Taiwanese immigrants' cultural toolkits are composed of the cultures from both their host and sending societies. In everyday life, individuals select various elements from this miscellaneous pool of values and norms to guide behavior and to give meaning to their social practices. In other words, their selections serve as the cultural tools of meaning construction, which vary in different contexts and when interacting with different people.[40] As Thomas Faist argues, immigrant culture is not a container that implies fixity and locality; rather, it must be considered a general human software or toolkit that suggests fluidity and spatiality.[41]

Studies of other middle-class Asian immigrants in the United States provide an outlook concerning both their similarities with and differences from the Taiwanese; they also help illustrate the unequal effects of pan-Confucian culture on Asian Americans' social practices. For instance, almost all studies of Asian immigrants describe a patriarchal nature of gender relations and family structure, especially among laborers and small family business owners. Most scholars use ethnic culture (e.g., Korean culture, Vietnamese culture, or Chinese culture) to describe the social norms and moral values in their studies, although some briefly discuss ethnic culture in terms of the historical roots in Confucianism. These Asian immigrant communities share many similar cultural characteristics, while each ethnic group also displays distinct characters because of their different political, economic, historical, social, and migration factors. In other words, Asian Americans are both culturally similar and different.

Manita Manohar's study of professional Indian/Tamil immigrant women in the United States provides a close contrast to the Taiwanese professional women in my study.[42] Manohar uses Indian culture to explain the traditions her subjects aim to cultivate within the next generation. The Indian values she mentioned are similar to those in Confucian culture, such as filial obedience and family importance—values that are also central to the Taiwanese tradition. Both Indian and Taiwanese professional women face cumulative disadvantage in the U.S. labor market, and neither of their families need dual incomes for survival. However, these two groups of women differ in their perceptions of employment. Indian women work to facilitate their families' upward mobility, while their Taiwanese counterparts work to find self-contentment and to alleviate their feeling of boredom from being home-makers during the early years of their family settlement. Additionally, Indian women's employment allows them to negotiate a greater share of domestic labor from their husbands, whereas most Taiwanese women do not succeed in such negotiations. Indian women make joint decisions about childcare and family budgets, while their Taiwanese counterparts predominantly control family finances and children's education.

Keumjae Park's study of Korean immigrant women provides another comparison. The professionals and small business owners in her study consider their employment necessary for family survival because of their husbands' downward mobility after immigration. They feel reluctant and ashamed about having to work because "based on my Korean values, men were supposed to be the bread-winners, and women were supposed to take care of the home," as one subject in the study said.[43] In contrast, professional Taiwanese women in my study find homemaking unfulfilling. Their families do not need the second income, and many husbands show strong opposition when their wives begin to think about finding a job. Regardless, these women choose to work outside of the home to enrich their immigrant lives.

Most notably, many Taiwanese couples bring economic resources given by both sides of the family when they settle in the United States. Usually, the husband's parents buy a house for the couple when he finds a job. The wife's parents give a great amount of cash for the young couple's emergency funds or simply as private money for the wife. Among the fifteen Taiwanese immigrant families in the area of my fieldwork, seven do not have to pay a mortgage because their parents purchased the house for them with cash. These families' privileged financial resources allow them to establish their middle-class American lives quickly with only one professional salary. Such an economic advantage also enables the wife to stay home without seeking additional income to advance the family's class status or to support the children's extra-curricular activities, as reported in Manohar's study of Indians and Park's study of Koreans.

The Filipina nurses in Yen Le Espiritu's study are yet another contrast to the Taiwanese and other middle-class Asian immigrant women. Many married female medical professionals in the Philippines enter the United States as the principal immigrants in their families. They often leave behind their husbands and children during the initial years of immigration, then bring their families over when securing permanent residency. As immigrant dependents, their husbands encounter disadvantages in the U.S. labor force. Many experience downward occupational mobility and consequently suffer from low self-esteem. Most couples recognize the importance of interdependence and having two incomes to achieve family prosperity in the new land. The employment of Filipina wives also leads to greater male involvement in household labor, mainly due to the wives' demanding job schedules in the medical field. However, women continue to shoulder most housework and childcare responsibilities.[44]

While Filipina wives maintain their professional statuses after immigration, most Taiwanese wives lose theirs and become housewives. Both Espiritu's and my studies reveal that women's earnings do not automatically lead to more egalitarian relations at home. For example, Espiritu points out that women's perceived cultural ideals about gender roles—men should be the breadwinner and the head of household—are a key factor in shaping their spousal relations. In my study, I argue that it is far more complex than just culture or gender ideology. Rather, various social and cultural factors interlock in varied ways to shape spousal relations in Taiwanese immigrant families (see chapters 3 to 5 in this book). Moreover, Filipina women express their admiration for the egalitarianism in Western culture and wish their husbands could do more. This is a sentiment that none of my Taiwanese subjects has mentioned.

In addition to comparisons with previous studies, my field observations documented some cultural differences between Chinese and Taiwanese immigrant women. For instance, there are two weekend Chinese schools in the area of my fieldwork, one run by Chinese and the other by Taiwanese housewives. At the Chinese-run school, a few mothers work with professional Mandarin Chinese teachers to manage the school. Most mothers just drop their children off at the school and pick them up afterwards. The professional teachers are in charge of the curriculum, teaching, after-school activities, and preparation for performances. In contrast, mothers at the Taiwanese-run school are highly involved in all aspects of school activities—from teaching to cleaning the classrooms. Before every Chinese New Year, Taiwanese mothers choreograph their children's dances, teach the dance moves, and organize and supervise weekly practices. They also design and often manually make the performers' customs.

The two schools also show distinctive performance styles for the Chinese New Year celebration—the most important local event to showcase Chinese culture to the larger U.S. community. The Chinese-run school always performs traditional Chinese dances, wears traditional Chinese costumes, plays Chinese musical instruments, and reads ancient Chinese poems—typical representations of traditional Chinese culture that the public audience stereotypically expects to see. In contrast, the Taiwanese-run school performs modern dance to popular music, including contemporary American, Korean, and Taiwanese songs. Their cowboy dance (illustrated in figure 1) exemplifies such a fusion characteristic of Taiwanese American cultural representation.

Moreover, the fifteen to twenty-five immigrant homemakers I observed at their monthly lunch gatherings show noticeable cultural differences between the two ethnic-Chinese groups. For example, Chinese women host their in-laws' visits only occasionally and for much shorter periods, while Taiwanese women often live with their in-laws for months. Chinese women also show more individualistic attitudes when talking about their in-law relations. Some state that their in-laws should not intervene in their

FIGURE 1. Taiwanese American boys performing at a Chinese New Year celebration

FIGURE 2. Taiwanese American girls performing at a Chinese New Year celebration

lives, and that they do not care what their in-laws say or think. In contrast, Taiwanese women demonstrate attitudes that are more traditional. Although many condemn their in-laws' unreasonable demands and express immense stress and anger about their in-laws' dominance, most still believe that daughters-in-law should be obedient and tolerant to maintain harmony in the household.

Interestingly, the difference between the two groups of women is quite the opposite when it comes to parenting. While both place a high value on their children's academic success, they exhibit different mothering styles. Chinese mothers are very strict and demand excellence in both academic and musical performances. Many do not allow their children to waste time on playing or hanging out with friends, and most of their children are in Ivy League colleges and play classical music in orchestras. In contrast, Taiwanese mothers are more laid back. They allow their children to play soccer, football, video games, and participate in track and field, musicals, and the marching band—activities that Chinese mothers consider "useless sports" and "low-class music."[45]

These variations among ethnic Asian immigrant women suggest that the extent of cultural effects on individuals' perceptions, attitudes, and behaviors is by no means homogeneous. Although influenced by the same cultural tradition of origin, immigrant women of different ethnic groups demonstrate both similarities and differences in their viewpoints and social practices. Using Orlando Patterson's concept, these women exhibit different *cultural configurations* shaped by various contextual factors, such as surrounding situations and power inequalities between the interacting parties.[46] The nature of immigrants' dual culture further complicates the structural factors that lead to women's choices as well as their rationalizations of those choices.

Place, Culture, Subjectivities, and Agency

Geographers have discussed substantively the importance of place in shaping immigrants' selfhood. They argue that movement between settings has a significant influence on people's subjectivities,

FIGURE 3. Ladies' lunch gathering: Taiwanese immigrant women

FIGURE 4. Ladies' lunch gathering: Chinese and Taiwanese immigrant women

especially those who migrate across national borders. In other words, individuals' self-concepts and social identities change with their geographic mobility.[47] David Conradson and Deirdre McKay use the term *translocal subjectivities* to describe immigrants' multiply located senses of self.[48] More specifically, immigrants' subjectivities are linked to two places: their sending and receiving countries. According to Faist, this transnational social field contains two systems of culture that sometimes offer contradictory values and norms.[49] For instance, Confucianism values women's submission, whereas Western ideology promotes individual autonomy. Cultivated by both cultures, how do Taiwanese American women (and other Asians) reconcile such conflicting messages in their transnational cultural schemata? What social factors affect which cultural elements they choose to define, understand, and interpret their lives? These interesting and complex social phenomena warrant sociological research.

Culture is central to meaning-making behavior, through which individuals present their subjective understandings of themselves and the surrounding social world. Unpacking such meaning-making processes helps us to understand not only subjectivities but also to reveal the underlying power relations that determine the meanings of social life. Nevertheless, culture is not the only factor that shapes human behavior. Rather, culture interacts with other structural factors, such as social class, gender, race, ethnicity, space, and migration history, to shape individuals' behaviors, perceptions, attitudes, emotions, and social practices. Giving explanatory primacy to culture or another single social variable would oversimplify the complexities of how intertwined structural factors affect individuals' lives in different social spheres and at different points in time during their life courses.

On the other hand, individuals are not simply carriers of culture or recipients of structural forces. They are competent social agents who actively negotiate meaning and resist structural constraints. As Giddens argues, the relations between social structure and individuals are dialectical, as social structure both constrains and enables individual agency.[50] Michel Foucault also asserts that "there are no relations of power without resistances."[51]

Gender scholars often discuss the notions of structure, power, resistance, and agency together because of their mutual presupposition and conceptual inseparability. Central to gender scholarship is the examination of how structural conditions place women in disadvantageous positions that constrain their choices. For instance, Judith Lorber and Barbara Risman both suggest that women's voluntary choices are socially constructed by the gender system; therefore, studying women's choices helps to reveal the social construction of gender.[52] Diane Wolf explains that agency is the reaction to structural constraints. She clarifies that agency takes various forms, including defiance, resistance, accommodation, passivity, and withdrawal.[53] In other words, exerting agency does not always lead to positive outcomes; it may sometimes change power relations or, at other times, it may reproduce structural inequality.[54]

Following these perspectives, I argue that women's choices and rationalizations for their choices provide rich data to uncover power and inequality in the larger social structure (not just gender, but multiple intersectional structural factors), its effects on individuals' lives, and how agency is exerted through their resistance against structural domination. In this study, I do not presume which elements of Confucian and American cultures are associated with subjects' lived experiences. Rather, my objective is to develop a deeper understanding of the women's subjectivities and selfhood as they are revealed in their life histories. As such, I take an inductive approach to analyze their narratives and uncover patterns of cultural and noncultural interpretations that emerged from the data. I pay close attention to power relations and their surrounding social contexts to examine the structural constraints on the women's lives and the varied ways the women exert agency in their resistance against power and in their meaning-making behavior. The stories Taiwanese American women tell in this book demonstrate not only the complexity of immigrant lives but also the multifaceted connections of gender, immigration, culture, race and ethnicity, citizenship, work, family, and the self.

3

Searching for Self in the New Land

I had nothing to do at home. I was bored to death! I worked
illegally as a babysitter, and I didn't care how much money I made.
I spoke little English and I did not have legal status [to work] yet.
But I didn't care. I just needed to get out of the apartment!
—Wendy, 54, computer programmer, former high school teacher in Taiwan

I was very unhappy every day. I couldn't feel myself at all. I was very
depressed, negative, and withdrawn. I was not trying anything.
Besides my life, I didn't really care anymore. I was so bored.
—Rose, 53, math tutor, former middle school teacher in Taiwan

My husband went to his lab early and came home late. I had
no one to talk to for weeks. I did not speak English, and I was
afraid to go outside.... I remember one day, I was sitting in my
dining room alone and felt I had forgotten how to talk.
—Linda, 53, homemaker, former nurse in Taiwan

As a high school teacher in Taiwan, Wendy enjoyed her job for
more than a decade, until one day her husband, Tim, decided to
relocate the family to the United States.[1] Tim came to the United
States in 1970 to pursue a master's degree in computer science.
Considering the separation only temporary, Wendy remained in
Taiwan with their two young children. However, before graduation, Tim applied for some jobs in the United States and received
several offers right away. Wendy recalled the difficult decision that
she faced: "I loved my job; I loved teaching; and I loved Taiwan. I

enjoyed my job so much that I honestly did not want to leave. . . . but it was such a great opportunity for Tim. I just couldn't say no. My kids hadn't seen their father for two years, and it would be terrible for them and our family if our separation continued. They needed their father. So, I quit my job and came here [the United States]. It was not easy for me, but immigration was the only choice I had for the sake of my family."

Wendy's story exemplifies how most middle-class Taiwanese immigrant families decide to move to the United States. Typically, Taiwanese men come to the United States to study. Upon graduation, they find jobs and persuade their families to relocate to the foreign land. Since the United States is an economically advanced Western country, most wives consider their husbands' employment as valuable opportunities and agree to come for a few years.[2] Even among couples who both pursue graduate study in the United States, it is usually the husband who wishes to stay while the wife plans to return. "Gaining some work experience for a few years" is a common argument. The family's temporary plan often turns into permanent settlement as the husband's career progresses. Meanwhile, once the children enter school, America's flexible educational environment in contrast to Taiwan's strictness adds another incentive for permanent settlement.[3] The family's continuing adaptation to and acculturation in the host society mitigates the stress and anxiety that accompanies initial immigration. Additionally, the spacious and comfortable living environment in a suburban area is a dream that would be impossible in overpopulated and polluted Taiwan. Over time, it becomes less and less possible for the family to return.

In other words, the settlement of middle-class Taiwanese Americans involves a process during which various factors are weighed when considering international migration. Very few subjects report a clear deciding point or a single motive for immigration, and almost all subjects consider return to always be an option.[4] This phenomenon exemplifies what Doug Massey calls *cumulative causation*: once immigration begins, different mechanisms, such as social networks and institutions, operate to shape the sustainability and perpetuation of international migration.[5] It also reaffirms that international migration is rarely a one-time action, but rather a developmental social process.[6] More important, I argue that this social process is not gender neutral. Rather, immigration and gender interact to create different work-family contexts in the lives of men and women and shape different opportunities, work trajectories, and life experiences.

For example, what happened when Wendy quit her cherished teaching job and moved to the United States to reunite her family? Becoming a housewife was her only option because of her dependent visa restrictions. In going from a highly respected teacher who loved her job in Taiwan to a stay-at-home-mom who spoke little English in the United States, Wendy felt lost. On the surface, her family was reunited after two years of overseas separation. But, on the inside, Wendy felt empty, unfulfilled, and desperate. I coin the term *housewifelization* to describe the phenomenon that international migration ties women closer to the domestic sphere and intensifies the work-family division. Based on subjects' life histories, I show that housewifelization not only restructures highly skilled women's lives and restrains their choices but also shakes and reconstructs their fundamental understandings of who they are.

In this chapter, I begin with a discussion on the gendering process of Taiwanese immigration by analyzing subjects' motives for initial migration and permanent settlement, as situated in their familial contexts. Next, I examine how the process of immigration intensifies the gendered division of work and family. Tracing the women's life histories, I document two diverged pathways that emerge in later years of their family settlement, how women's perceptions of employment, housework, and themselves are challenged in this process, and how the women's well-being is consequently affected.

International migration as a developmental social process can be illustrated by individuals' motives for initial immigration and permanent settlement.[7] Since the process of immigration involves economic, social, cultural, and psychological risks, the decision to relocate to a new society is an important step and a drastic change for individuals and their families.[8] Immigration motives reveal the context of immigration considerations and how individuals' social locations (e.g., gender, race/ethnicity, social class, marital status) affect these considerations. Immigration motives also implicate many important and meaningful sociological issues such as structural push-pull factors, gender and family relations, household economic strategies, and social networks.[9] Thus, analyzing immigration motives is the first step in understanding an immigrant group's presence in the host society. It provides a foundation to acquire in-depth knowledge concerning how the social actions of immigration affect individuals and their families in the settlement process. While several scholars have examined individual motives for immigration, few have discussed their gendered meaning and consequent effect on women's and men's lives.[10] As immigration is a gendered social process, it is important to examine gendered motives for immigration and their influence on immigrants' adaptation experiences.

Immigration through education characterizes the major pattern of Taiwanese immigration to the United States. That is, most immigrants from Taiwan originally come to the United States to study; they later settle permanently when they find jobs after graduation. Regardless of this general pattern, men and women differ significantly when considering permanent settlement. While most Taiwanese immigrant men decide to stay in the United States permanently for job opportunities, women's settlement decisions overwhelmingly rely on noneconomic considerations, such as family reunification, children's education, political stability, and living environment. Even among those female subjects who initially come to the United States to study, not all of them settle for careers. In my previous study, 70 percent of Taiwanese immigrant men initially came to the United States to study, and 68 percent of all male subjects settled for job opportunities. In contrast, 53 percent of Taiwanese immigrant women came to study, and only 29 percent settled for job opportunities.[11] This finding suggests that men's immigration journeys show a more linear progress, whereas a large portion of women have varied considerations when it comes to permanent settlement.

The following excerpts exemplify the varied explanations that middle-class Taiwanese immigrant women provided concerning their decisions to settle in the United States:

My kids were suffering in Taiwan's schools. As you know, Taiwan's educational system is very competitive, so kids have a lot of homework and exams every day. My son was very outgoing and energetic when he was little. But, starting in middle school, he became very anxious and unhappy. He studied, studied, and studied just about every minute. He brought his alarm to bed, worrying about not finishing his homework or not doing well on the tests the next day, because he would be beaten up by his teacher if he didn't do well at school. My daughter was in elementary school at that time. One day she was hit by her teacher because she forgot to bring crayons to school. When I saw the bruises on her hands, I was very upset. I called her teacher and asked about the hitting. Her teacher questioned my concern and said, "Well, your daughter was not the only one that I hit. Other parents did not complain. Why are you questioning me about this? What's the big deal?" At that moment, I knew we had to leave. It was not easy for us because we were already over forty and had worked for a long time in Taiwan. It was not easy to start over in a foreign country, but I was determined to leave for my children's education and well-being. (Eliz)

Taiwan was very unstable because of China's threats. You don't know when China would initiate a war. . . . I was scared of Communists. I thought if we stayed in the United States, we would be able to save my parents if China were to take over Taiwan. (Dolly)

I just wanted my family [to] stay together, no matter in Taiwan or here [in the United States]. My husband decided to settle in Chicago, so it was very natural that we stayed and built our life here. (Mindy)

I came to study. I was in a master's program of education. Then, I met my husband and got married. Unexpectedly, I was soon pregnant. At that time, my husband had just found a job and become a permanent resident. We didn't have any relatives here and had to rely on ourselves. I was only two courses shy from earning my degree, but I had to take care of my child. So, I never finished my studies, and it's still a regret. Life is very unexpected and it does not always turn out the way that you planned. (Elena)

I came to study. When I applied for the green card, it was primarily for convenience, because I needed to work and earn money. I did not think of settling in the United States at all. My plan was to return after graduation. Besides, I love my country very much, and I never thought of becoming American. But then I realized that my husband had already decided to stay here permanently. He wanted to stay, and I didn't mind staying. (Tracy)

There are not many research institutes in Taiwan. Most jobs for PhDs are teaching positions at universities. I like doing research but not teaching, so I thought I would have more opportunities here [in the United States] than returning to Taiwan. (Cindy)

As revealed in these narratives, women's decisions to permanently settle in a foreign country involve various considerations. In fact, female subjects usually report multiple motives when explaining why they decided to stay in the United States, while most men offer only one major reason (i.e., pursuing their own careers). This pattern is particularly evident for subjects who were married at the time when assessing the family's settlement plan. In most Taiwanese immigrant families, the husband is the primary decision maker for the family's relocation. As I report elsewhere, more than 60 percent of Taiwanese husbands make the decision to permanently settle their families in the United States. Close to one-third of the couples jointly make this decision, and only 6 percent of Taiwanese wives play the role as primary decision maker for the family.[12]

In other words, it is fairly typical among Taiwanese immigrants for the husband to come to the United States for graduate studies, and then for their wives and children to follow from Taiwan. Many single men get married in Taiwan after completing their studies and securing jobs in the United States. They then bring their brides to the new land to begin their family lives. For those Taiwanese students who meet their spouses while studying in the United States, it is usually the husband who decides to stay, and they often look for jobs before graduation. When determining whether settling in the United States would be best, the wife considers several factors, such as living environment, family well-being, and the prospects for the next generation.

These gendered incentives and contexts in which married men and women consider their settlement decisions shape different paths for their lives from the onset of their immigrant journeys. For instance, male subjects work in the professions in which they were trained in graduate school. In contrast, most female subjects work in fields different from their professional training because they did not earn their degrees in the United States or are not fluent in English. In this study, about half of the subjects (twenty-three women, approximately 51 percent) earned their final degrees in the United States, whereas almost all of their husbands or ex-husbands (forty-three men, approximately 96 percent) earned their advanced degrees from U.S. universities. Many women discontinue or delay their employment when they migrate as dependents. These women are also pulled away from their parents and close friends in Taiwan, while many men invite their parents and siblings to visit or live with them in the United States.[13] The next sections document the varying work-family contexts that immigration creates in highly skilled women's lives and their influence on the women's self-concepts and well-being.

Intensified Gendered Division of Work and Family

For any new immigrant, visa status is a key factor that affects work and family. In the United States, foreign workers need to have a valid H-1B visa to maintain their legal employment. This work permit is usually sponsored by their employers and must be renewed every three years. Foreign workers' spouses and children can apply for an H-4 dependent visa when the worker applies for the H-1B, which allows the family to stay in the United States legally. However, the H-4 visa does not permit employment. With employer sponsorship, foreign workers can also apply for permanent residency—the green card—for themselves and their dependents. Holding a green card allows individuals and their dependents to work legally and reside permanently in the United States. They can also apply for citizenship as soon as five years after acquiring the green card.

Theoretically, for a married couple, the husband and the wife can each apply for a H-1B visa when they find jobs. In the case of Taiwanese immigrants, the husband typically lands a job first, which prompts the family's settlement consideration. When applying for his H-1B visa through his employer, the husband also applies for H-4 visas for his spouse and children. As most families initially plan to return, the wife usually does not seek employment following immigration unless she also studied in the United States. In other words, the husband often serves as the pioneer who plants the roots for his family's settlement. Once the husband's employment is secured, the family begins to sketch their plans, including the wife's decision to work or to stay home.[14]

This family immigration strategy often situates the wife in a vulnerable position. Many women give up their cherished jobs so their families can stay together. When immigrating as dependents, the women cannot work before acquiring permanent residency. In the early phase of their settlement, they are often at childbearing age or already have young children at home. These circumstances largely constrain married women's choices for themselves. Uprooting from the society in which they grew up and moving far away from their parents, the women face many drastic changes that can be financially, socially, culturally, and psychologically challenging. While some immigrant wives consider this transition as a break from work, many struggle to handle feelings of emptiness, loneliness, and loss of purpose.

LEAVING CAREERS AND LOVED ONES BEHIND

For women who gave up their jobs in Taiwan in order to reunite their families in the United States, it is difficult to talk about their careers prior to immigration. While many find their immigrant lives full of adventure and excitement, some deeply miss the pride, fulfillment, and independence they experienced in the professions that they gave up decades ago. As Mary described:

> I gave up my job as a prosecutor to accompany my husband. There were very few female attorneys in Taiwan at that time [1960s], so my parents were very proud of me. I had a bright future ahead of me, so my parents were very disappointed when I decided to come here [to the United States] to be with my husband. I was very naïve back then. I thought once a woman is married, she should follow her husband and consider her husband's well-being as her priority. So I quit my job and came here. I thought we would return to Taiwan after my husband finished his PhD. I gave up everything I had in Taiwan. My career, my parents' expectations, everything. . . . I hate that I'm a woman. If I were a man, I would have stayed in Taiwan. I would have made my parents proud by pursuing my career. But, as a woman, I need to prioritize my family's well-being.

Mary moved to Wisconsin when her husband, Greg, was completing his PhD in public policy in the early 1960s. She soon started working in a school cafeteria, washing dishes and cleaning tables to support Greg. Unexpectedly, Greg failed to finish his degree and the couple felt too embarrassed to return to Taiwan. Greg left school to work for the state government, and Mary found a job as a computer programmer after taking a few courses at a community college. She worked very hard and continued to advance her programming skills by attending all of the training sessions her company provided. Without a U.S. degree, Mary still succeeded in her programming job and retired as a manager.

In contrast, Greg changed his jobs every few years, while Mary stayed in the same job until retirement. During our interview, Mary complained about how Greg's carelessness and unreliability had ruined their marriage. Recalling what she gave up four decades ago and what she went through after immigration, Mary was overwhelmed by feelings of regret and bitterness. She attributed her misfortune to her gender and Confucian teaching:

> I was very traditional back then, you know. I was raised in a very traditional family. Growing up, I was taught all the Confucian values. I was taught that women ought to be obedient to their fathers, their husbands, and their sons after their husbands die. My father brought many classic Confucian books from China when he migrated to Taiwan in 1949, and I read them all in high school. All those books tell you stories about how wives sacrifice themselves to help their husbands succeed, and how loyal they are to their families. I was instilled in all those traditional ideas when I was young. Since my husband was my first boyfriend, I thought I should be dedicated to him no matter what. I was too naïve. I did not even think about whether or not our personalities suit well. Back then, I just felt I was ready to sacrifice myself for him and devote myself to his success. So, I walked into this dead-end marriage for forty years.

Despite her unhappy marriage and the challenging role as the primary breadwinner, Mary was quite successful in her job as a computer programmer and had several good friends from work. She also taught her two daughters the importance of independence, autonomy, and egalitarianism. After retirement, Mary turned to Buddhism to find inner peace.

Mary's story exemplifies the *misemployment* many highly skilled Taiwanese women experience after immigration. Similar to Mary, whose status changed from a promising prosecutor to a cafeteria worker, many subjects took blue-collar jobs in their early years of family settlement, both legally and illegally. For instance, Dolly was a teaching assistant at a private college preparing to become a lecturer in Taiwan, but worked as a waitress after moving to Chicago; Wendy was a high school English teacher in Taiwan, but worked as a babysitter after immigration; Sophia was an accountant in Taiwan but worked as a babysitter, cafeteria worker, maid in a hotel, and change girl in a casino in Delaware. These women's education and professional training did not match what they did in these blue-collar jobs. However, these jobs were available choices of employment for them under the structural constraints that they faced during the early years of their immigrant lives.

Katie, another immigrant who became a computer programmer in the United States, shared a similar life trajectory with Mary. Katie's husband, Jeff, immigrated through the sponsorship of his sister, who owned an upscale Chinese restaurant in downtown Chicago. After visiting his sister in the summer of 1976, he applied for U.S. citizenship and worked at her restaurant. Two years later, Jeff asked Katie and their daughters to come to the United States. Katie described the ambivalence she felt at the time:

> I loved my job [in Taiwan]. I had been working since sixteen as an accountant assistant at Customs. I was very respected by my boss, coworkers, and my clients. I had so many good friends in Taiwan. So, when my husband decided to relocate our family to the United States, I was devastated. There were so many things that I had to give up: my friends, my parents, everything that I had enjoyed my entire life. . . . If we stayed [in Taiwan], we would have had a good life. I had a good job that had great retirement benefits, and I could have been able to see my parents

often. If you ask me now, I am still not sure if it was a right decision to come here. . . . Maybe I should have had insisted that we stay.

Overcoming feelings of uncertainty, Katie and her daughters joined Jeff in 1982 for the sake of their family well-being. After her daughters entered school, she began to take computer courses at a community college and then worked as a computer programmer for a university. Although fairly successful at work, Katie was heartbroken when her husband had an affair and asked for a divorce. She raised her two daughters alone and continued her job at the university for almost twenty years. She had several good friends at work and enjoyed the simple life that she and her daughters shared in Chicago.

These immigrant women leave behind not only their careers but also their loved ones. Although not everyone grieves over the jobs that they gave up prior to immigration, most subjects miss their families a great deal. Many are unable to visit their elderly parents as often as they wish, and a few miss their parents' funerals. In particular, housewives lack the financial resources to frequently travel overseas. Moreover, while many Taiwanese immigrant men invite their parents and relatives to live or visit with their families in the United States, married women seldom do so. Even when both sides of the family visit from overseas, the husband's family usually stays much longer than the wife's because of Taiwanese patriarchal customs. The husband's parents also tend to impose traditional gender roles on the wife, which becomes a major source of distress for married women (see chapter 5). Overall, the journey of international migration brings more hardships to married women than to men.

STARTING THE IMMIGRANT LIFE

Migrating as dependents restricts immigrant women's employment opportunities. Unable to work, most women who hold dependent visas endure overwhelming feelings of loneliness and isolation during the early years of settlement. For former professionals who worked daily, dressed well, and enjoyed the respect, status, and income that accompanied their jobs, becoming a homemaker in a foreign country is a radical change that often brings feelings of boredom, isolation, and loss of purpose. For instance, Rose graduated from one of the best teachers' colleges in Taiwan and taught for three years at a middle school before immigrating with her husband, co-owner of an international importing company. Although they owned a million-dollar house in a gated community, living alongside upper-class White families, Rose was unhappy. She described what she endured during those early years after she arrived in the United States: "I was very unhappy every day. I couldn't feel my self at all. I was very depressed, negative, and withdrawn. I was not trying anything. Besides my life, I didn't really care anymore. I was so bored. . . . For many years, I wished I could return to Taiwan. At least I would have my own job and my own money, and I could be independent." After struggling with boredom and negativity for more than a decade, Rose began to volunteer as a math tutor at a community center. She soon became the most popular tutor at the center and found a sense of fulfilment in helping students. Many students asked her to tutor them on a regular basis, and she began teaching students at home for a small fee. For Rose, the self-worth and respect she regained from tutoring was priceless.

Similarly, as described at the beginning of this chapter, Wendy gave up her high-paying and highly respected teaching job in Taiwan to reunite her family when her husband found employment in the United States. Although Wendy believed that it was the right decision for the family, she struggled with boredom and loneliness for years after arriving in Chicago. She recalled: "I had nothing to do at home. I was bored to death! One day, I saw an ad in a grocery store in our neighborhood. Someone was looking for a babysitter. I took the job. I made very little money and it was illegal, but I didn't care. I just needed to get out of our apartment. I spoke little English and I did not have legal status [to work] yet. But, I was so bored that I would do anything to be able to go out!" At first, Wendy's husband opposed the idea of working, because they had young children at home and did not need additional income. Working illegally also posed risks for the family. However, Wendy was going crazy at home, feeling bored and useless. Determined to work, she kept looking for jobs. Despite her husband's opposition, she found a babysitting job in the neighborhood that allowed her to bring her kids to work. She went to work with excitement every day and considered it a valuable opportunity to learn English because she needed to communicate with the couple about their expectations. Making little money was never a concern for Wendy. When babysitting, she learned English by reading children's books and watching cartoons with the baby. She also imitated how the couple spoke English and observed how they arranged things around the house. Wendy diligently prepared her conversations with her employers and enjoyed the sense of fulfillment her job provided.

After obtaining her green card several years later, Wendy longed for more challenges. She found a data entry job at an information technology company but chose to work only night shifts to ensure that her employment did not affect her roles as wife and mother. She went to work after her husband came home in the evening. Although she earned minimum wage—despite her college education and professional background—Wendy enjoyed the time outside of her home. Her intelligence and dedication quickly earned her opportunities to work on different computer systems and to receive advanced training offered by the company. Wendy also took several computer and English courses at a community college. Eight years later, she became a computer programmer with her own cubicle at work and good benefits.

During her early stage of settlement, Wendy overcame many obstacles, such as her initial language barrier, visa restrictions, and balancing household responsibilities. She also had to show her husband, Tim, that she was not neglecting her duties as mother and wife, and that she was unhappy being a homemaker. Tim's attitude changed from resistance to understanding after seeing Wendy's suffering, determination, and devotion. Many highly skilled women go through the same struggles when they decide to enter the U.S. labor force. Gaining support from their husbands is particularly crucial in achieving their goals. Many women manage to find employment in practical areas such as computer programming, accounting, and real estate, although these jobs differ significantly from the women's previous professions in Taiwan.

Regardless of many successful stories, not every woman experienced a smooth negotiation with her husband when deciding to return to work. A few women's spousal relations deteriorated when they began to prepare themselves for employment. Dolly revealed her dark moments in the process of finding fulfillment in her immigrant life:

> After we came to the United States, I realized that I did not
> have my own world. I had only my husband's world. I was very
> unhappy, so I decided to take some courses at a community
> college. I took English and computer courses, and I worked [illegally]
> at a Chinese restaurant in order to practice English and
> have something to do. I began to have friends from school
> and work, and sometimes I went to parties. However, my husband
> didn't like that I worked and that I had my own friends.
> He blamed me for not being a good wife because I did not just
> stay home cooking and cleaning. We argued a lot, and he started
> hitting me. Then, he became more and more violent. He even hit
> me when I was pregnant. One day, I had bruises all over my face
> and my nose and mouth were swollen. I looked at myself in the
> mirror and felt so ashamed. . . . I hid myself at home and did not
> want to go out. At that time, I had already had some friends, but
> I was afraid of telling anyone. I thought they would think I did
> something wrong to anger my husband. It was the first time that
> I thought about killing myself. . . .

Fifteen years of abuse and suicidal thoughts consumed a huge part of Dolly's life, leaving inerasable scars on her self-esteem and mental health. Before immigrating to the United States, Dolly worked as a teaching assistant at a private college in Taichung, Taiwan, and planned to pursue a master's degree in accounting and become a college lecturer. She was the first in her family to earn a bachelor's degree, so her father had high hopes for her future. Nonetheless, international migration not only changed her career plans but her abusive marital relationship also crushed her sense of self-worth. Not giving up her dream, Dolly eventually got a divorce and worked as a licensed real estate agent. At the time of our interview, Dolly appeared to be a confident professional and an energetic woman. She was also in a healthy new relationship, and her children were in college and quite successful academically.

Another subject, Stacie, also struggled with her ex-husband's expectations of a submissive wife. Soon after getting married, her then-husband asked Stacie to bring slippers, make hot tea, cook dinner, and get a hot tub ready for him every evening. Although Stacie and her husband both worked full time, Stacie was expected to shoulder all of the housework and serve her husband dutifully. However, doing housework was much more difficult than studying or working for Stacie who had always been career-oriented. Overwhelmed and unhappy, Stacie ended her marriage of three years and had remained single ever since. A breast cancer survivor, Stacie commented that fighting cancer was easier than the battle with her chauvinist ex-husband. After the divorce, she earned a master's in business administration and worked as a computer programmer.

HOUSEWIFELIZATION OF HIGHLY SKILLED WOMEN

While many subjects find jobs sooner or later after obtaining permanent residency, not all of the women are able to work. Bandana Purkayastha refers to the *cumulative disadvantage* that highly skilled immigrant women encounter in the host society.[15] The obstacles faced by immigrants include a great loss of social and professional networks; not all credentials and education in the sending county are transferable or recognized in the U.S. job market; learning a foreign language in adulthood is challenging, not to mention speaking fluently enough to handle a white-collar job; having young children at home not only delays immigrant mothers' entry into the U.S. labor force but also consumes their energy to a large extent. When adapting to the host society, many immigrant mothers have to navigate the educational system for their children and explore local sociocultural resources for their families. Even when highly skilled immigrant women successfully enter the U.S. labor force, they stumble upon glass ceilings in the workplace and struggle to balance their work and home lives. Because of these various factors, a great number of immigrant women choose to become full-time homemakers regardless of their high education and professional training.[16]

In other words, international migration housewifelizes highly skilled women. Both visa restrictions and cumulative disadvantage tie married women to the domestic sphere after immigration and intensify the work-family division. The thirty-three professional subjects in this study spent two to fifteen years being homemakers before they reentered the U.S. labor force; and less than one-third worked in the fields for which they felt a true passion. All the twelve housewives were professionals in Taiwan, and never returned to work after immigration. Some of them wished to work, but were discouraged by the cumulative disadvantage they had to overcome to find employment in the host society. Housewifelization not only changes the women's work trajectories in the host society but it also affects how the women think of their roles in the family, the purpose of their employment, and their place in the new country.

Linda was a nurse in Taiwan prior to immigration. When her husband decided to pursue advanced study in the United States in the early 1990s, she fully supported him because it would significantly enhance his career prospects in Taiwan. In order to accompany her husband, Linda quit her job and moved to Virginia where her husband's graduate school was located. She devoted herself to taking care of her husband. Considering her unemployment only temporary, Linda believed that she could easily find a job upon their return. Like many foreign students' wives, Linda did not see the need to learn English or find illegal employment during her husband's student years. Day after day, she cooked, cleaned the apartment, and waited for her husband to come home from his lab. This was a time when the Internet was not prevalent, and international phone calls were expensive. Linda sometimes wrote letters to her parents and sisters, but she only talked about good things in order not to worry them. In reality, she was depressed and devastated:

> My husband went to his lab early and came home late, usually around midnight. I had no one to talk to for weeks. I did not speak English and did not understand what's on TV. I was afraid to go outside because there were many Blacks in the neighborhood and we did not have a car. I remember one day I was sitting in my dining room alone. After staring at the same wall all day long, I suddenly felt I had forgotten how to talk, so I started to panic. I felt I couldn't breathe. . . . I was panicking. . . . You know, I am a very outgoing and talkative person. Usually, I am very good at adjusting my mood. But at that moment, I was so anxious that there might be something wrong with me. . . . I worried that I may have become mentally ill. I was a nurse, so I knew something was not quite right with me. The minute my husband came home that night, I screamed and started crying for hours. I just couldn't stop [crying]. . . . I was so scared [chokes up].

The hardship continued for almost a decade, until Linda's husband found a steady job after finishing his PhD. During these difficult and lonely years, the births of her daughters helped soothe the feeling of emptiness, although her social isolation did not change much. Linda kept busy with her children as a way to cope with her depression. Although living under the same roof, their daughters rarely saw their father. Linda's husband was largely absent in their family life because of his demanding workload and job insecurity due to his immigrant status. Linda remembered one day her husband came home to have lunch with the family. Not recognizing their father, their daughters thought a stranger had broken into their home. They screamed loudly and hid together behind a sofa. Recollecting her memories of the old days, Linda said in a sad tone:

I was so isolated and lonely. . . . But I couldn't tell anyone how difficult life was, because everyone [back in Taiwan] thought we were living the American dream. I did not want my husband to worry about me because his work was very stressful. Being a foreigner [immigrant], you've got to work much harder than others in order to survive. And there's racism at work that he faced every day. It was not easy for him, either. So, I just swallowed the hardship and took one day at a time. Life was never that difficult for me [choking up]. Growing up in a wealthy family, I was my parents' precious princess. I had everything, and my life was wonderful. But the first ten, or maybe twelve, years here [in the United States] were extremely difficult. Looking back, I still don't know how I survived that [time].

After Linda's husband secured an academic job, their family settled in a small suburban area and lived a comfortable middle-class life. With no hope to return to Taiwan or to work again, Linda devoted herself to her family. She learned how to cook various Taiwanese dishes, volunteered at her children's school, and taught at the Chinese school that her children attended on weekends.

Regardless of their education and past professions, immigrant wives who are not prepared to live in a foreign country encounter significant obstacles in the host society. Another highly educated housewife, Gina, described the depression she endured during her first year in the United States: "I started crying the moment I got on the plane. I cried almost every day during my first year in the United States. It was so hard. . . . all the cultural shock. . . . I didn't understand what's on TV, and I didn't have any friends. And my mother-in-law lived with us. . . . I cried myself to sleep every night. It took me a very long time to get used to the [immigrant] life here."

The language barrier is a common issue that prevents immigrant housewives from fully embracing their American lives. Immigrants do not always follow the news in the host society, and they are often afraid to speak English in public. This language barrier also constrains communication with their children's teachers and other parents. Immigrant women are also subject to everyday racism because of their lack of fluency in English and their foreign accent (as discussed extensively in chapter 6).

In addition, middle-class Taiwanese immigrants usually reside in predominantly White suburban areas. Ethnic-Chinese organizations often exist in metropolitan areas to serve the needs of immigrants, but very few Taiwanese associations can be found in small towns, especially in the Midwest region. As a result, a number of Taiwanese immigrant wives have limited access to coethnic networks, and many are unable to participate in coethnic organizations when their children are young and need their full-time attention. Although social isolation is common, many form small social circles with fellow immigrant women to exchange information and provide social support. Sharing the objective to immerse the next generation in Taiwanese culture and language, immigrant mothers often collectively organize weekend Chinese schools where their children can learn Mandarin Chinese and Taiwanese culture. They work as teachers and help with various tasks at the school. In fact, weekend Chinese schools serve as more than a language school—they provide immigrant housewives with a place where they can use their talents, knowledge, and passions. Many immigrant mothers devote themselves to organizing Chinese schools and teaching the next generation. They also establish close networks with other families through these Chinese schools.

DIVERGENT PATHWAYS AND THE
MEANING OF WORK AND HOUSEWORK

Two major paths exist for highly skilled Taiwanese women who settle in the United States: some work in white-collar occupations, while others become homemakers. International migration not only shapes the work-family contexts of both groups but also affects the meaning of paid work and housework in the host society. In this study, most professional subjects worked in high-demand fields, such as computer programing, accounting, and statistics, which differ from the subjects' original fields of study. The change in profession gives work a different meaning. For homemakers in a foreign country, the family is the center of their lives, and their children's achievements become a major source of satisfaction. The following sections discuss how the two groups of women talk about the meaning of paid work and housework as well as what they imagine themselves doing if they had not migrated to the United States.

Immigrant Women in White-Collar Professions. During the early phase of settlement, usually the first decade of immigrant life, common hardships for highly skilled Taiwanese immigrant women include adjusting to the new environment, getting used to their new status as a racial minority, and unemployment. While ten of the thirty-three professional subjects worked in the professions for which they had trained, more than two-thirds of working women in the study chose jobs outside their fields of study. The majority spent several years as homemakers because of visa constraints, a phase during which the women underwent intense searches for meaning and sense of self. Many asked themselves the following questions: Who am I in this country? Do I want to work? Should I find a job that is practical, or should I stick to my previous profession? Do I want to be a homemaker forever? How can I use my education, skills, and talent here? What do I want? Is the immigrant life fulfilling for me?

In these questions and their searches for answers, the women's narratives shift from a cultural model to a self-initiating, practical, and more self-centered discourse. Before immigration, the cultural values of Confucian womanhood—the prioritization of husbands' careers and family well-being—dominated the women's decisions to relocate. After immigration, visa restrictions engender a profound sense of *lost self* and extensive questioning among many career-oriented women. This structural constraint not only changes the women's roles in the family, workplace, and community, it also largely contributes to gendered experiences of immigration and adaptation. While their husbands continue to pursue their careers after completing advanced studies in the host society, the women's radical change of status from career women to foreign housewives requires tremendous adjustment.

Furthermore, most women are of childbearing age in these early years of settlement. Many have young children who need much attention, while their husbands enter the racially disadvantaged labor force. These circumstances complicate their new lives as immigrants. While some (ten out of thirty-three) continue their previous professions, many find jobs in new fields. Usually, the women enroll in college courses or earn second degrees after their children enter school. They choose fields with high demands in the U.S. labor force, such as computer programing, statistics, and accounting. For these women, the meaning of paid work differs significantly from that of their previous professions in Taiwan. As Mindy pointed out, "Here, what I have is a job, a job that brings income. It is not a career." Nevertheless, working outside of their homes means so much to them that the subjects do not mind choosing this practical route. Many accept low-paying, entry-level jobs at first, but eventually climb up the corporate ladder to become professionals. Their determination to work overcomes the obstacles created by international migration.

No matter what professions they choose, most subjects enjoy the autonomy, independence, and income that accompany their jobs. Several have become managers in their companies and supervise many employees at work. What the professional subjects have in common is their enthusiasm for work. Although facing disadvantages due to their gender, race, and immigrant status, the subjects often confront their work-related issues with courage and progressive actions that contradict stereotypes of Asian women, as illustrated in chapter 6.

Suburban Immigrant Housewives. Although only twelve women were homemakers in this study, all professional subjects had spent varied time (two to fifteen years) being stay-at-home moms during the early phase of their family settlement, primarily because of their visa restrictions. Like many suburban housewives across the country, middle-class Taiwanese immigrant homemakers center their lives around the household and their kids. Their typical day starts with making breakfast and lunch for the family. After the kids go to school, they clean the house, do laundry, or go grocery shopping. They often surf on the Internet, watch Taiwanese shows or Korean soap operas on satellite, or chat with coethnic housewives over the phone.[17] Some volunteer at their children's school a few days a week. Immediately after the kids come home from school, the mothers transport them to tennis, soccer, chess, piano, or violin lessons. Following these after-school activities, they make dinner for the family, while the children do homework or play in the backyard. On weekends and during school breaks, many families take short trips out of town. Some visit Taiwan every few years to see relatives and friends or have visitors from Taiwan from time to time.

Most homemaker subjects in this study read Taiwanese news online on a daily basis and closely follow social and political events in Taiwan. In other words, these housewives usually know much about the current state of Taiwan, including its pop culture. Many continue to identify with Taiwan even after becoming U.S. citizens for decades. Their exposure to American culture is often through the next generation. For instance, teenagers often bring cultural information to their immigrant mothers through the American pop music they listen to, movies they watch, and activities they do with friends. These homemakers also socialize with non-Asian parents of their children's friends, but very few have close friends outside of their ethnic group.

As Akiko Yasuike observes in her study of highly skilled Japanese immigrant housewives, women's weak economic power contributes to a clear breadwinner and homemaker division of labor in the family.[18] Immigrant housewives are not only tied to the domestic field, they are also more likely than their employed counterparts to apply traditional gender-role expectations to themselves. Regardless of their previous professional statuses, most homemaker subjects believe that housework is their sole responsibility, not only because they are unemployed but also because they are aware of the racial inequalities their employed husbands may face in the workplace. Therefore, providing a secure and comfortable foundation for the family is perceived as their main responsibility. As Frances commented:

> A very long time ago, I once wondered if I was useless being a housewife. Then, a friend said to me, "Do you realize what a wonderful life we have? Our husbands have to face racism at work and they have to work super hard to secure their jobs because of their immigrant status. And you see, we can just stay home, chat over tea, and make these desserts together. How fortunate we are!" I suddenly realized that everything has its trade-off. Although I'm not employed, my family is my work. It's the foundation for our family's survival in a foreign country. If I do my work well, then my husband can focus on his work, and then our family would prosper.

Many scholars have observed the importance of having a stable family for immigrant women as a foundation to resist racial inequality in the larger society, even when the women have to accept certain patriarchal arrangements in the family.[19] This is also true in middle-class Taiwanese families in which the wives are homemakers. Middle-class Taiwanese immigrant housewives consider their primary responsibilities to be maintaining clean, warm, and stable homes so that their husbands can concentrate on work and the family can prosper. Almost none of the housewives ever asked their husbands to do housework, unless the husbands volunteered to help. In most families, the husbands do yard work but not housework, and they are not responsible for supervising their children's homework unless they are asked.[20] In families that draw a clear gendered division of labor, however, the wives are often overwhelmed by their household and childcare responsibilities, especially those with young children. Christine described the exhaustion she felt: "I often iron my husband's shirts and pants until midnight. He needs nice clothes for work, and it's my job to have them ready for him. Oftentimes, I am so exhausted after my three kids go to bed. Then I think, no, I can't sleep yet, I have to get those shirts done. But I'm so tired, so sometimes I cry while ironing."

In another family, Gina's husband routinely did the dishes and took over childcare responsibilities after work. He also encouraged Gina to go back to school when their children were in elementary school. Although she earned a graduate degree in accounting from a prestigious research university, Gina believed that her place was in the family and never looked for a job. Gina's husband, Liam, respected her wish to stay home and continued supporting her in other ways, such as being involved in their children's activities. Liam's family background largely shaped his egalitarian attitudes. His father passed when he was very young, so, growing up, he and his brother helped their widowed mother around the house. For Liam, helping with housework had been a natural thing to do his entire life. In contrast, Gina was raised in a traditional patriarchal three-generation household. Her father made all of the decisions and her mother was a submissive homemaker and daughter-in-law. Influenced by her family culture, Gina firmly believed that she should dedicate herself to Liam's success and her children's well-being. She explained that having a stable and strong family was particularly essential for her husband to succeed as an immigrant. Therefore, she remained fully devoted to her family and rarely spent money on herself regardless of her husband's high income and strong support.

Like Gina, almost all of the housewife subjects share the mentality that "because I do not bring income to my family, I cannot spend money on myself." While fairly generous with investments in their children's education and extracurricular activities, these immigrant housewives are very cautious with money they spend on themselves. They prioritize their children's and their husbands' needs over their own. In addition, feelings of uncertainty due to their immigrant status also contribute to cautious spending. They know how to find good deals and save money; many manage their families' financial investments and carefully monitor their stock trades online. Women's perceptions of their roles in the family not only reveal their sense of self but also largely affect their spousal relations and how they negotiate power in their marriages. In chapters 4 and 5, I discuss gender relations, gender ideologies, and gender practices in the Taiwanese immigrant family.

Nostalgia and the Imagined Self. At the end of every interview, I asked the subjects the following question: "What do you imagine yourself doing if you did not settle in the United States, but stayed in Taiwan instead? What would you have become?" Professional subjects who worked in occupations different from their original fields replied almost immediately: "I would have had a successful career in the field that I love." Their distinction of "the career they loved in Taiwan" and "the job they do in the United Sates" is clearly drawn in response to this question. In contrast, professionals who continued to work in their trained fields described the obstacles that they would have encountered in Taiwan:

> Taiwan is a place where you need networks to get good jobs. I don't have that, so it would be difficult for me to have what I have here [working as a manager in the United States]. (Tracy)

> In Taiwan, women are devalued. I would not have been given equal opportunities. Here, as long as you work hard and show your competence, you can do as well as men. (Cindy)

> Maybe I would not have been too different if I returned to Taiwan, in terms of what kind of job that I do. But I would have been hesitant to speak up for myself at work because women are expected to be quiet and passive [in Taiwan]. Here, I can express my opinions more freely and have more independence. (Ann)

This gendered view of employment opportunities provides a contrast to how professional subjects perceive the intersectional constraints of race, gender, and foreign-born status in the white-collar workplace (see chapter 6). Because Taiwan is a single-race society, gender constitutes a major cause of structural inequality, whereas issues of racial discrimination and anti-immigrant sentiments are prominent in the United States. Subjects' narratives show their clear awareness of the different structural factors in both societies that could confine their employment opportunities and career success.

When responding to the same question, middle-class housewives often paused and pondered for a few minutes before depicting the lives that they imagined had they not immigrated to the United States. Here are some examples of their answers:

> I would have become a successful professional woman if I had stayed in Taiwan. I have an MBA from a U.S. university, which would give me a head start in Taiwan's job market. I might also have chosen not to get married and not to have kids because of the competitive environment in the business world. In marketing, you need to give 120 percent in order to be successful. I enjoyed working, and I enjoyed making money [laughing]. So, I would have become a workaholic if I were still in Taiwan. (Christine)

> I would have gone back to work as a nurse. It's impossible for a family to have only one income in Taiwan [because of the low salaries across the board]. I was the best in our hospital back then. I was already the head of our unit before we left Taiwan. (Linda)

> I really wish I had stayed in Taiwan. At least I would have had my own job and my own money, and I could have been independent. I loved teaching, and I graduated from one of the best teaching universities. I would have become a high school teacher, teaching the subject [math] that I have so much passion for. (Rose)

> I would still have my dream job working as a financial consultant and have a lot of money. (Michelle)

As these housewives pictured the lives that they would have had, their narratives show an *imagined self* centered around employment. The construction of their imagined selves not only reveals the careers that they thought they would have had and the dreams they once embraced, it also evokes a wave of nostalgia. They yearn for a lost piece of self in time and space, ponder a different work trajectory, and wonder about choosing a different route in life. The imagined self links memories of their current and past selves as well as the contrasts between the two; it conveys a sentiment of nostalgia that feels both familiar and remote. These women's sense of nostalgia also signals the presence of a dynamic cultural value system. Before immigration, they strongly believed in the importance of adopting traditional gender norms—prioritizing family well-being over their own careers. After decades of being housewifelized as a result of immigration, the women fantasize what they could have accomplished in their former professions. In this imaginary context, pursuing a career and not getting married seem to be perceived as being just as culturally appropriate. This imagined self downplays the stigma associated with single women in Taiwan, a society that continues to value Confucian gender culture in modern times.

None of the women said that they would choose to become a homemaker. Lost career opportunities seemed a prevalent regret among the housewives, although they did not necessarily dislike their immigrant lives in the United States. Some made light of their lack of achievements as a result of international migration, while others stressed their regrets:

All my friends in Taiwan are doing very well. Many are already mangers and have a lot of money. I have nothing [smiles]. I have accomplished nothing. (Gina)

I would have been a very popular professor had I stayed in Taiwan! When I taught English in Taiwan, my students loved me. I would have become a college professor and would have a very colorful life. Here, I am nobody. (Kelly)

My daughter often jokes about how I have achieved nothing here [in the United States]. She said I'm wasting my life being a housewife. But my kids are my life. Their achievements are my achievements. As long as they are happy, I'm happy. (Linda)

Gina and a few others mentioned their successful peers in Taiwan in a contrast to accentuate their lack of accomplishment in the Unites States. It is possible that not every old friend in Taiwan is successful, but these women's selective comparisons reveal a sense of grief over their lost careers and their imagined selves had they not immigrated.

While acknowledging their sacrifices, these housewives found satisfaction in their children's accomplishments. All housewives emphasized the importance of their children's achievements and family well-being when asked what they found pleasing about their American lives. They said they embraced the simple life in the United States where they had nurtured close family bonds, which are difficult to develop in Taiwan where other social obligations and pressures often take over family time. Because Taiwan is a small island where people reside close together due to space limitations, social involvement is much greater and extended kinship relations are much closer. For example, Taiwanese people often receive invitations from acquaintances to attend weddings, funerals, and social gatherings. When their relatives or friends need something (sometimes money), people are asked and expected to help. Living far away from their relatives allows immigrants to have some social space, which excuses them from these expectations and obligations.

Furthermore, both professionals and housewives share the deep sorrows of not being able to see their parents, siblings, and close friends frequently because of the distance created by international migration. A few were unable to visit when their parents passed away or became terminally ill, leaving deep regrets and sadness in their hearts. In other words, the physical distance that exempts immigrants from social obligations also restrains their access to social support and connections to loved ones.

Conclusion

As renowned scholar Steve Gold once wrote, "The decision to relocate one's self, family, and community to a new setting and society is one of the most drastic social actions people may take during their lifetime."[21] International migration involves taking various social, economic, cultural, and psychological risks, which may not always be a smooth process. As shown in the Taiwanese immigrant case and previous studies conducted in various countries, international migration generates a negative effect on highly skilled women's careers; it also creates a clear breadwinner and homemaker division of labor in middle-class families.[22]

In the case of Taiwanese, patriarchal Confucian values initially factor into married women's willingness to give up their own careers to prioritize their husbands' career advancement and their family well-being through immigration. Upon overseas relocation, the legal categorization of Taiwanese wives as "dependents" under the larger patriarchal and heteronormative contexts of U.S. immigration policy becomes a major structural factor that maintains the gendered nature of immigration adjustment and the gendered work and family relations for Taiwanese women. Many highly educated, highly skilled Taiwanese women become homemakers, at least during the early phase of their settlement. Constrained by their dependent visas and various adaptation obstacles in the host society, the women are tied closer to the domestic sphere and the work-family division is, thus, intensified—a gendered process I call *housewifelization*. While a few embrace the break from paid work, most women struggle with overwhelming feelings of boredom, isolation, emptiness, and loss of purpose. Mourning their lost careers, the women intensively search for a sense of self and redefine the meaning of employment and housework in the new land. In other words, while culture serves as the foundation of Taiwanese women's decision to become housewives in the initial phase of their immigration, visa status constitutes a major structural factor that foregrounds their housewifelization process.

Two common pathways are taken after the initial phase of settlement: one group overcomes their cumulative disadvantage and reenters the U.S. labor force, usually in practical fields such as computer programming and accounting; and women in the other group remain homemakers for the rest of their lives. The former considers their paid work as a job that brings income, rather than a career that fulfills their dreams and passions. Still, the women find contentment in the independence, autonomy, and income that their white-collar occupations bring, and enjoy the time working outside of their homes. The latter shoulders all household and childcare responsibilities and considers maintaining a stable family as their priority. Satisfaction is found in the next generation's achievements and close family bonds that are difficult to develop in the sending society. Both groups of women endure hardships resulting from international migration, while adjusting their perceptions and plans in their immigrant journeys. Their imagined selves reveal a sense of grief over their lost careers and a sentiment of nostalgia. Encountering the drastic changes in their new work-family contexts created by immigration, the women's resilience is manifested through various forms of agency as they adapt to the new surroundings.

4

Negotiating Egalitarianism

I often iron my husband's shirts and pants until midnight.
He needs nice clothes for work, and it's my job to have them
ready for him. Oftentimes, I am so exhausted after my three
kids go to bed.... so sometimes I cry while ironing.
—Christine, 39, MBA, homemaker

I work full time as well, so of course he should do housework, too.
—Tracy, 52, MA, manager at insurance company

My husband is not very good at cleaning. Every time he cleans
the bathroom, I'd have to do it over. It's easier that I just do it
myself. I am better than him so I do most housework.
—Elena, 56, BA, director of public services

I am in charge of our family finances. My husband is not very good
at math. So, of course, it's me who makes financial decisions. There's
no need to discuss with him. I just make decisions for us.
—Judy, 39, PhD, professor

Christine's narrative, as seen in the beginning quote of this chapter, exemplifies how homemakers typically think of their responsibilities. Given the high socioeconomic status of her family, Christine could easily afford to hire help. However, she insisted that housework and childcare were her duties because she was a stay-at-home mom and her husband had a busy full-time job. Christine repeatedly said during our interview, "Housework is my job."

Nevertheless, daily work consumes enormous energy, and Christine expressed the overwhelming exhaustion she felt without any help. Day in and day out, Christine took care of three young children, did all the housework, went grocery shopping, transported her kids to tennis lessons and soccer games, and volunteered at her children's school three days a week. Her husband, Paul, did almost nothing around the house because, as Christine cited Paul's words, he "was too busy with his work and career."

When I asked why she did not ask her husband to help, Christine explained:

Paul thinks I'm home all day, so I have plenty of time to do housework. He doesn't help at all, even when I ask. He thinks it's my job, not his. Sometimes, when I don't have time to cook, he gets angry and blames me for not doing my job. It's extremely frustrating and exhausting because I don't have any help at all. You know what? I have to iron everything, including his T-shirts and shorts, and, I have three little children at home. My husband does nothing to help. Even when I'm sick, the dishes would pile up in the sink for days. He would not touch a dirty dish. Sometimes I'm so mad. But, I'm the one who is unemployed. I feel I'm not in a position to blame him. I know he is very busy with his work, and his work is very important.

In other words, employment status creates a clear boundary between work and family and defines the scope of the couple's responsibilities. For more than a decade, the strict division of labor in her marriage continued and became a way of life. Christine described a scene that vividly illustrates the absence of her husband's involvement: "It was a summer time when we were leaving town for a family vacation. A friend came to take us to the airport. So, we were loading on the driveway. I put the car seats on and put my kids into the van, then went back to the house to bring out all our stuff. There we were, on the driveway with several heavy suitcases. My [female] friend helped me move one suitcase after another to the car, and my husband just stood there watching us the whole time. He did not even move a finger!" I asked whether she had asked her husband to help. She said "No" and explained, "He'd say I was the one who planned family trips [because it was considered a domestic task], so I was responsible for all trip-related work. I did not even bother to ask him for help. It's just the way we do things in the family."

Her life as a housewife and mother of three kept Christine busy all the time, leaving no room for relaxation. Regardless, she insisted on not hiring help although her family can afford a babysitter and a housekeeper. She explained, "I'm not bringing any income to the family, so I should not spend money on this [hiring help]. It is my job to take care of my kids and maintain a clean home." In spite of Christine's strong will and determination, having three kids under age seven is not easy for any young mother. Her oldest son had some behavioral issues and often got into trouble at school. Without any help from her husband or anyone else, Christine's daily life was extremely stressful. One day, all three children were cranky, crying, and fighting with each other while Christine was making dinner. Suddenly, Christine broke down and screamed for several minutes. The next day, she went to her family physician who prescribed her an antidepressant. In tears, Christine described her feeling of desperation: "My body began to feel weird because of all the negative emotions and exhaustion. I told my doctor how I felt and all the difficulties that I was facing. My doctor asked me about my relationship with my husband, and I said he [my husband] never helped with housework or the kids. And then, I began to cry. . . . I just couldn't control myself. . . . so my doctor suggested that I take medication." During the seven months Christine was on medication, she continued to shoulder all of the childcare and housework duties alone. Her husband was accustomed to a life without doing anything at home. Christine continued to insist on not hiring help because she deeply believed that housework was her sole responsibility. The medication helped her stay calm, but the burden remained.

Christine had a very close relationship with her mother, and they talked on the phone every week. However, she did not mention her burnout or medication to her mother. When I asked why, she said: "No, I don't tell my mom. I can't. My mom would be very upset and she would worry about what's going to happen to me if my husband wants to divorce me. Every time my husband and I have an argument, she would think it must be my fault. She always tells me that I should be obedient and tolerant [to my husband]. It's very difficult for me that I can't tell my mom how I feel in my marriage. But, I don't want her to worry. I don't want her to worry that I might be abandoned [by my husband]." Christine was not the only one pressured by her own mother to abide by traditional gender norms. Many married women's mothers condemned their daughters for their nonconformity to Confucian gender culture, which I illustrate in detail in chapter 5.

Christine's story might sound extreme, but the lack of sharing in housework between husbands and wives is fairly prevalent in Taiwanese immigrant families. Among the over 100 Taiwanese-immigrant households I have come to know, either through interviews or fieldwork in the past decade, approximately 15 to 20 percent of the husbands shoulder an equal share of the housework. While some professional women hire help, homemakers usually consider housework their sole responsibility, even when it becomes overwhelming.

Regardless of such unequal division of labor, it would be wrong to assume that Taiwanese immigrant wives are powerless in the family. In fact, many wives—including Christine—were solely in charge of their family finances, although they were not the primary breadwinners. They were also entrusted with most decisions concerning children's education and family social activities. The power issue in spousal relations is far more complicated than a single sphere of family life can fully portray.[1]

In this chapter, I document subjects' explanations of how labor is divided in the family and why; I also explore who makes decisions about family finances and why. Women's accounts of these two issues provide important information about their gender ideologies, gender practices, and strategies for negotiating egalitarianism.

These accounts also reveal spousal relations and dynamics in the family.

Gender Relations in the Taiwanese Immigrant Family

Married women's abilities to negotiate equal partnerships with their husbands depend on several factors. Scholars in the sociology of the family usually apply resource theory to discuss spousal power relations. According to resource theory, women's social and economic resources have a positive effect on their status at home. That is, more socioeconomic resources lead to higher status and more decision-making power in the family.[2] Numerous scholars of the immigrant experience have followed this thesis to examine how married immigrant women's employment in the host society affects their spousal relations. Findings from previous studies about Dominicans, Vietnamese, Koreans, Mexicans, and Filipinos are consistent in that employed women gain greater bargaining power for domestic labor and family budget responsibilities because of their greater financial contributions to the household.[3]

The case of Taiwanese Americans provides a contrast to the literature. Employed or not, many Taiwanese immigrant women solely or jointly control the family economy. Although the majority of these women shoulder most of the housework, many provide practical reasons, rather than gender norms, to explain their division of labor. Below, I synthesize subjects' narratives when justifying how the couples perform two household tasks, domestic labor and financial management.

LABOR DIVIDED

When subjects explained how they divided household labor and why, two different rationalizations emerged: (1) culture-based interpretations: labor is divided according to the traditional gender norm, and (2) practical reasoning: labor is divided based on spouses' employment status and housework skills. Below, I illustrate these two logics in the women's accounts.

Culture-Based Interpretations. As introduced in chapter 2, Confucian gender role expectations ascribe women's place in the domestic sphere. Therefore, it would be no surprise if this traditional culture were used to explain women's greater share of domestic labor. Unexpectedly, less than one-third of the women used culture to explain why they did most of the household work. When a cultural explanation was given, the women described their housework as a natural gender division of labor, something they took for granted and had little to say about. The following narratives illustrate this rationalization:

> Traditionally, housework is the wife's responsibility. I feel I'm obligated to do housework. It should be my work, sure thing. (Marcia)

> I do most of the housework because it's the natural duty of a married woman. It's my job. (Joy)

> Of course I do all the housework. It's my job being a wife and a mother. (Ruth)

> My husband does nothing [at home], it's our culture. (Mary)

> Sure, I do all the housework. It's my job as a wife. (Patty)

These women considered the traditional gender division of labor—women are responsible for housework and childcare—an unquestionable norm. For instance, Patty stayed home for almost ten years after migrating to the United States. When she thought about taking courses at a local community college to prepare for a professional job, she made sure that she finished all of the housework and scheduled her courses around childcare responsibilities. She felt she had to show evidence to her physician husband that going back to school would not affect her roles as mother and wife. Keeping family her priority, Patty also felt less guilty about pursuing employment. Similarly, Wendy was bored at home during the early years of settlement and desperately wanted to work. She took a data entry job and volunteered to do night shifts. In doing so, Wendy convinced her husband that her employment would not affect her household and childcare obligations. Neither of these women complained about the burden of shouldering all family responsibilities. Socialized in Confucian culture, these women display a sense of *domestic self* in their gender ideologies and gender practices.

In contrast, men and mothers-in-law often used Confucian gender culture to justify men's exemption from domestic work. Some men considered guys doing housework a shame. Therefore, even when they did help sometimes, they tended to conceal it to save face in front of others. Many men actually believed that housework was women's work, even when their wives worked full time. For instance, Stacie and her ex-husband, Brent, both worked full time as professionals. When they were married, Brent strongly believed that married women should take care of their husbands. He asked Stacie to bring him slippers, serve him hot tea, and get a hot tub ready when he came home from work—requests that Stacie was surprised to learn only after they got married. At first, Stacie tried to do what was asked, but constantly struggled with their traditional gender practice. She described her feelings:

> Now I look back, I know it was not right that he asked me to do so much. Back then, I didn't really know what went wrong. I just felt overwhelmed, exhausted, and that I was feeling very depressed. He wanted me to take care of him dutifully. But, he did not want me to quit my job and become a stay-at-home wife because he liked having this additional income. I did what I could. . . . typing his reports for him, cooking, cleaning, making desserts, and taking care of our then one-year-old daughter all by myself. I wanted to see him succeed, so I did what I could. I tried, but, honestly, I was not very good at housekeeping. Every tiny little thing around the house took me a lot of effort, and I was very slow when doing housework. So, I was miserable.

Stacie's feeling of misery exploded when, one day, Brent teased her about the food she made and the unsatisfactory cleaning work she performed. The couple began to argue more often and finally decided to get a divorce when their daughter was three. Stacie recalled her ambivalent sentiments three decades ago:

> I felt I was not suitable for being a wife. I struggled to do what he asked. I am very good at studying, but I suck at house-keeping [embarrassed smile]. . . . I felt so miserable that I just felt I couldn't do it anymore. I just did not want to live with him anymore. I couldn't take it anymore, you know? He was a nice person, but he said really mean and hurtful things. I couldn't take the verbal abuse. It was very hurtful. . . . maybe I was oversensitive, but I felt so upset that I went to see a psychologist. I felt so sorry and guilty to him that I asked for a divorce. . . . but I just couldn't take it anymore!

Seeing a psychologist helped Stacie realize that it was not her fault that she asked for a divorce, and it was not her fault that she did not meet her ex-husband's expectations. Gradually, she learned to forgive herself, and she became more independent. She also felt relieved that no one was there to criticize her housekeeping skills any more. Since her divorce, Stacie had a few relationships, with both White and Taiwanese men, but she remained single because she had "lost trust in marriage" (Stacie's words). Regardless of the difficult past, her struggles with breast cancer, and her emotionally distant relationship with her daughter over the years, at the end of our interview Stacie expressed strong feelings of happiness, independence, and self-love.

Dolly also had a husband who demanded traditional gender practice. Her husband, Rob, often criticized her, saying that she was not a good wife or good mother because their home was messy and she did not prepare a hot breakfast every day. During the early years of their family's settlement, Dolly wanted to explore the world outside of her home by working part time (illegally) at a Chinese restaurant. Rob opposed this and demanded that she remain a homemaker. Dolly used the potential financial gains to convince Rob, and she finally found work as a waitress on the weekends. However, as Dolly began to meet friends and enjoy working outside of the home, Rob felt ignored, and the couple argued more often. Finally, their heated arguments turned into physical fights. Dolly was beaten frequently whenever her husband was angry, even during her pregnancies. Rob also hit their two boys as a means of discipline.

When Dolly talked to a few close Taiwanese friends (both male and female) about her husband's violence, they all suggested that she tolerate his behavior and stay married. "They said fighting is normal in Taiwanese families, it's no big deal. They also told me to save face for my husband by not telling people about it," recalled Dolly. When she shared her story with a White friend, she was again advised not to tell others because it would affect how the White community perceived her children. Finally, Dolly turned to the pastor of her church for help because she was extremely unhappy. However, her Taiwanese pastor's advice was to forgive Rob and remain loyal and dutiful in her marriage because, as her pastor said: "This is what God would want you to do."

Dolly stayed married, endured the abuse, and struggled with self-blame for fifteen years. The unspeakable pain consumed her emotions, energy, and health, but Dolly held on to a dim hope because her inner self voiced something different from all the advice she received from people around her. During those years, Dolly attended numerous self-empowerment workshops, read self-help books, and continued to search for her true sense of self. Little by little, Dolly nurtured her inner strength and cultivated her self-growth. Finally, in 1997, she filed for divorce and began to rebuild her life. At the time of our interview, Dolly was a licensed realtor and in a healthy relationship. She showed a strong sense of independence, and she enjoyed her single life. "The scar is still there, but I am strong," Dolly said to me with a tearful smile. After our interview, she gave me a warm hug and thanked me for listening to her life story. As we embraced, I felt her incredible resilience, and her gentle yet strong spirit.

A few women used culture to explain why their husbands did not do housework, and they empathetically accepted the status quo. For instance, Kristi explained that her husband grew up in a very traditional family, in which his father and all of the boys never did any housework. As a result, her husband was used to not doing anything at home: "It's not his fault [that he is not doing anything]. It's how he was raised. He has been so used to not doing anything his entire life. It's very difficult to change that [habit]. I don't blame him."

Such gender norms and practices, shaped by patriarchal Confucian culture, are best illustrated in three-generation households. In these families, parents-in-law tend to demand traditional gender roles from the couple. They consider men doing housework a violation of Confucian gender norms and, thus, condemned their daughters-in-law for not fulfilling their gender roles when they needed help. As Blair said: "My mother-in-law would get really angry if she sees my husband doing housework. She thinks it's women's job and that I am not doing my job well if I need help from my husband or others." Another housewife, Rose, described the enormous cultural pressure on both her and her husband:

I do 100 percent of the housework, especially during our first ten years of marriage. When we bought this house, my parents-in-law came to stay with us for six months every year. I had to do a lot of work around the house. My older son was still little back then. One day, he was cranky and crying recklessly. I was holding him with one hand and cooking with the other. I kept looking at my husband, hoping he'd help. But he did not dare to move even a bit! We looked at each other, and I saw the fear and worries in his eyes. If he held the baby for me, his parents would be very angry. He is a filial son and did not want to anger his parents. I had no help at all. So, I just took my son everywhere I went, even when going to the bathroom.

Not only Rose's parents-in-law, but also brother-in-law's and uncle-in-law's families frequently visited her house and lived there for varied periods of time, ranging from a few weeks to several months each visit. Rose did and was expected to do all housework, including all her in-laws' laundry. Her husband's family was very wealthy, but hiring help was never considered because the daughter-in-law was supposed to fulfill her duty. Because nobody helped or offered to help, Rose was often sick as a result of the exhaustion and stress. When I asked why such a gender practice seemed nonnegotiable, Rose explained, "Well, it's our culture. Nobody had ever questioned anything, and no one thought there's anything wrong about it."

Rose's husband, Ethan, co-owned an importing company. She and her family lived in an upper-class gated community, alongside many entrepreneur millionaires. Rose initially came to the United States to pursue a master's in mathematics education, but did not finish her degree because she became pregnant during her first semester of study soon after marrying Ethan. After her son was born, Rose wanted to return to school, but Ethan asked her to stay at home to take care of the baby because he did not trust babysitters. In fact, with her in-laws' frequent visits during their early years of settlement, Rose could not do anything else but housework and childcare. She was extremely unhappy and found no meaning in life (also see chapter 3).

More than ten years later, when her two children were in high school and her in-laws' visits were less frequent, Rose asked to take ESL (English as a Second Language) courses at a local community college. Ethan supported her because he thought learning English would help Rose adapt to their upper-class American life. Very soon, Rose discovered various opportunities in the outside world. She was excited and wanted more than just learning English. She asked Ethan if she could take some professional courses, such as accounting and computer programming, and to work as a volunteer math tutor at the community center. Ethan opposed and was furious about the idea. He said Rose's spending more time on school and volunteer work would interrupt his life and career path because she would have less time to devote to her family responsibilities. Rose turned to her two teenaged sons for support. Finally, the three together convinced Ethan to let Rose try a few courses by promising no disruptions in Rose's domestic duties.

Similar to Rose's family, households in which traditional gender norms are highly regarded and enforced by the husband and his parents do not allow married women's employment status to excuse them from the cultural expectations of Confucian womanhood. Housewives and working women alike are expected to dutifully do all housework and serve in-law guests. For instance, Katie, Jen, and Nicole all worked full time, but they shouldered most of the housework and served their in-laws on a daily basis. In these families, the mothers-in-law forbad their sons to do housework and blamed their daughters-in-law if they asked their husbands to help. In other families, husbands secretly did housework when their mothers were not looking and secretly showed support to their overburdened wives. In the next chapter, I discuss in-law relations and dynamics under Confucian culture.

Practical Reasoning. Employment status and housework skills are two rationales that most women used to explain their division of domestic labor, what I call *practical reasoning*. As illustrated in Christine's story, employment status creates a clear territorial boundary between work and family, which defines the range of the couple's responsibilities. Like Christine, all housewives in the study considered family-related matters their sole responsibility because they were home every day and they did not have paid jobs. Many said, "housework is my job" and "childcare is my responsibly" because they were not employed, and their husbands did not have time for housework because they worked full time. In other words, unemployment status shaped a sense of *domestic self* in these homemakers' perceptions of their roles and of who they are.

Moreover, a few mentioned the importance of maintaining a clean house and a stable family because they understood the obstacles their husbands faced at work due to their race and immigrant status. This rationale is illustrated in the following narratives by two housewives:

It's very difficult for immigrants to succeed. My husband works very hard. Being a foreigner [immigrant], you have to work much harder than others to succeed. And, there's always racial discrimination at work. I understand what my husband is facing every day, so it's my job to make sure that he doesn't have to worry about anything at home or about the kids. (Linda)

My husband spends most of his time doing research. So, our family and the children are my responsibilities. He works very hard and has established his career here. It has not been easy. He has to work harder than others because he is a foreigner [immigrant]. So, I don't want him to worry about housework or the kids. I want him to be able to concentrate on his work. (Gina)

Previous studies of immigrant women have reported similar sentiments. Although gender inequality remains in many immigrant laborer families, it is considered less severe than the racial inequalities and racism in the larger society that both immigrant men and women face. As a result, married women tend to choose to unite with their husbands and male counterparts. Therefore, having a stable family serves as the foundation for resisting racial oppression in the outside world.[4] Similarly, middle-class Taiwanese immigrant women mentioned the importance of having a stable family because immigrant life is hard.

Every woman I interviewed placed a high value on family. Nevertheless, that does not mean that they would stay in their marriage by all means. Six women divorced their controlling husbands, two of whom were violent, after struggling to maintain stable families for years. At the time of the study, all of these divorcées had lived in the United States for over two decades. After their marriages were dissolved, these women never thought about returning to Taiwan as they would have had to face the stigma attached to divorced women in Taiwanese society. Moreover, by the time of the women's divorces, their children ranged in age from seven to twelve and had all entered school. Therefore, it would have been difficult to leave their children behind or take them to Taiwan, where the children would have had to adjust to a completely different educational system, culture, and language. Molly explained how she and her children thought about the possibility of return: "My kids didn't want to go back to Taiwan [after my divorce]. They said teachers in Taiwan hit students, so they didn't want to go to school there. I think the culture is very different there. If we go back, people would laugh at me. We have migrated to the United States, and everybody [in Taiwan] envies that. It'd be a shame if we return. I would not know how to explain why I failed [as an immigrant and as a wife]. So, I thought, we'd better stay here." Meanwhile, these women embraced the freedom and autonomy of being single in the United States. The following quotes illustrate their feelings of emancipation:

I don't want to go back to Taiwan. Divorced women are considered a shame there. I don't want to bring the shame and social stigma to my parents. I feel I'm such a failure. I don't want to disappoint my parents. Maybe because I failed my marriage, I have devoted myself to my work and have greatly enjoyed it. Unlike marriage, at work, as long as you work hard, you'd gain something. I feel very satisfied with my work, and feel I have accomplished a lot. I would not be able to achieve the same had I returned to Taiwan after my divorce. Here, nobody would judge you just because you are divorced. (Stacie)

Now is the happiest time in my life. Ever since my divorce, I have grown a lot. Now I know what I want for my life, and I'm working hard to pursue my dreams. I want to go back to school and get a PhD. I want to become a teacher. I feel so content and conscious about myself. I find my life very fulfilling now, even though I suffer from back pain and some other health issues. I don't feel the [psychological] pain anymore like I did in my marriage. Now I know how to nurture my inner self. I'm glad I got a divorce. Now I can live my life freely. If we did not migrate, we would have stayed married because of all the social pressure there [in Taiwan]. Even the Taiwanese community here [in Chicago] is very conservative. I am very different and atypical from them [other Taiwanese immigrants]. I am very liberal. So, I am thankful that I got a divorce, so I have an opportunity to grow and to gain such a deep understanding of myself and of my life. The world outside of the Taiwanese community is so free and full of possibilities! (Dolly)

I don't want to go back to Taiwan. What can I do in Taiwan? I want to stay here [United States]. My life is here, and my kids are here. In America, divorce is no big deal. It's a healthier society [than Taiwan]. A lot of people are divorced. There are many self-help books that instruct you how to cope with divorce and sadness. So, I'm lucky that I'm here. I can easily find resources in the library about how to help myself recover [from divorce]. I exercise, go to concerts, and find projects to do on weekends. I'm enjoying my life here. (Rachel)

These narratives show that the dissolution of marriage led to opportunities for independence and self-growth. The women had also adapted to their American lives and enjoyed their singlehood in spite of the initial financial hardships and psychological struggles that resulted from divorce.[5] Liberated from Confucian gender norms, the women gained much greater freedom, autonomy, and self-contentment after their divorces. They obtained a deeper understanding of themselves and the purpose of their lives. In other words, the broken marriages in some ways shaped these divorced women's sense of wholeness.

As mentioned earlier, housewives used employment status to justify the strict gender division of domestic labor along the work-family line. In fact, many employed women used the same logic to negotiate a greater share of the housework from their husbands, although none of their negotiations succeeded. For instance, Sue was a fifty-six-year-old pharmacy technician. For almost three decades, she was exhausted with her full-time job, raising three children, and serving her mother-in-law who lived with her family for eleven years. Her husband refused to do house-work, and he was protected by her mother-in-law who demanded traditional gender practice. Sue explained:

> I do most of the housework. My husband goes out to play Ping-Pong almost every night, so I have to do all the work. Sometimes, I complain that he's not helping and it's a lot of work for me. I work full time and have three children to raise. I'm tired after work, but I still have so much to do around the house. . . . It's very tiring, and he does not help at all. I devote everything to my family and my children and am just exhausted every day. . . . that's why I couldn't finish my master's [in accounting]. I didn't have time and energy to study! I have lived in the United States for more than thirty years, but have never been to a movie. . . . you just work, work, and work, for your family and children. You'd forget about yourself. My children are my everything. I don't think of myself or what I want anymore.

Sue's husband owned an apartment complex in the neighborhood and often worked on the property, including cleaning apartments after tenants moved out. Nevertheless, he had never done any cleaning at home because "it's women's job" (Sue citing her hus-band's words). Sue's mother-in-law reinforced this value by impos-ing Confucian gender expectations on the couple. She criticized Sue for not fulfilling her role as a wife every time Sue asked her husband to help. Sue expressed her exhaustion repeatedly during our six-hour interview, naming all the sacrifices she had made for her family and recalling all the dreams she had when she was young. Like Sue, four other women did not finish their studies because of the heavy load of housework and childcare during their graduate student years. As a result, they all changed their job plans to prioritize their family duties. These women expressed a sense of loss and regret when they talked about their unfinished advanced degrees, mourning the careers they could have had. A piece of their *lost self* was buried in the dreams they once embraced.

Tracy was another professional woman who used her employment status to negotiate with her husband without success. A manager at an insurance company, Tracy was extremely busy at work. She was also active in the Asian American community, and she devoted herself to training members of the younger generation to be leaders. Despite her success at work and in the community, Tracy was overwhelmed by the second shift and was upset with her husband's lack of sharing. She expressed her frustration and disappointment:

> My husband encouraged me to participate in social activities because he thought I am a talented leader. He is very supportive of that. Especially the core mission of this Asian American organization is very close to my heart. I want to help the younger generation succeed. So, I am very busy both at work and after work with all these responsibilities. But, I still have to do housework. He would not help, you know. . . . he supports me, but I still have to do what I have to do [housework]. . . . For a very long time, I tried to convince him to do more. I once thought that I could get him to do as much as I did because we both worked full time and it's only fair. But, after a while, I gave up. I stopped wasting my time [on the negotiations]. Life is too short. I didn't want to waste more time on feeling angry about it. . . . So, I hired help. . . . one to clean the house and the other does yard work. I just couldn't continue to waste my time.

For employed women, the second shift is often a challenge. Being immigrants, they do not have relatives who can lend a hand like many native-born Americans whose extended families live nearby. Many struggle to balance work and family, especially when their children are young. Professional jobs demand a great amount of time and energy, and shouldering housework and childcare with little help only adds anxiety and stress. Many subjects expressed their feelings of exhaustion. Like Tracy, about a half of the dual-income families outsourced the burden by hiring help. Some also tried to lower their expectations of housework. However, for those employed women who lived with in-laws, neither hiring help nor having their husband's help was an option. Therefore, their stress and anxiety was multilayered (see chapter 5).

In addition to employment status, household skills were another common justification that subjects used to explain their division of labor. For instance, many subjects commented that their husbands did not clean well or did not know how to cook, so they did most of the housework. "My husband doesn't like cleaning," Elena said. "I don't like him to do the cleaning either because he is not very good at it, especially cleaning the bathroom. Every time he cleans an area, I'd have to do it again because it's never clean. And, when I say 'it's not clean,' he would respond: 'I think it's clean.' So, anyway, I feel. . . . I'd just clean it myself. It's easier, and I like to do the cleaning."

Similarly, Rebecca said: "My husband is not very good at cleaning and cooking. He would do it if I ask him to, but he is not good at all. So, I do most housework." A few professional women (Tara, Alice, and Eliz) also said, "My husband doesn't know how to cook and how to clean, so I do most housework." They seemed to take for granted that who did what around the house was determined by the talents they possessed—also a common rationale that many of the women used to justify why they managed the family finances, which I discuss later in this chapter.

Unconventional Husbands Who Do Housework. Very few Taiwanese immigrant husbands do housework, except for yardwork. Among the few families in which the husband does housework, the couples' equal share of labor began early in their relationships and went through few changes over time. Among these couples, all the wives had earned their advanced degrees in the United States and worked full time in professional jobs. Interestingly, all these women used *unconventional* to describe their husbands and implied that their families' gender division of housework was atypical. They were aware of their unusual arrangement, which violated

Confucian cultural norms, and sometimes joked about how they deviated from other Taiwanese, as the following interview narratives reveal:

> We share housework. My husband cooks, so I have time to relax after work and talk to my kids every night. My husband is not very traditional [laughs]. . . . we are very egalitarian, and this kind of relationship allows me to do what I do [focus on work accomplishments and work long hours] and become who I am today. We communicate a lot and are supportive to each other. He is very different from most Chinese [and Taiwanese] men I know [laughs]. (Lauren)

> We met when we were graduate students here [in the United States]. Being a foreign student, you've got to be very independent. We both did housework back then, and have continued the lifestyle after we got married. There was never a discussion about who did what. But, I know we are very different [from other Taiwanese immigrant families]. (Cindy)

> My husband does a lot around the house and with the kids. He often cooks and is a better cook than me [laughs]. But, I feel bad for him when other Taiwanese husbands mock him about that. At our social gatherings, people sometimes joke about how he is the only [Taiwanese] man who does housework. They make it sound like a noble thing, but you can tell it's more like a teasing. He [my husband] is very atypical. (Jamie)

These comments point to the husbands' divergence from traditional Taiwanese gender practice. These women showed appreciation for their spouses' equal share of housework, but at the same time they were aware of the cultural deviance of their families. No subject mentioned American culture as the rationale or inspiration to practice egalitarianism. They also engaged in little or no negotiation as their husbands had been doing much of the housework since the beginning of their relationships.

Many previous studies report married immigrant women's greater control of their family budgets as a result of their employment in the host society. These women gain more power in the family mainly because of their greater economic contributions after immigration.[6] In contrast, most women in my study managed their family finances either independently or jointly, regardless of their employment status. Many housewives dominated family financial decisions although they did not bring home any income. None of my subjects complained about not having control over money or needing their husbands' permission to use money. Rather, some joked about their powerful and sole control over family budgets, even though they were not the primary breadwinners.

Why? Similar to subjects' explanations of their division of household labor, most women used practical reasoning (employment status and skills) to justify their dominance over family financial decisions. For instance, Christine was exhausted by housework and childcare responsibilities because her husband did nothing around the house. Nevertheless, she was entrusted with 100 percent decision-making power in managing her family's finances and stock investments. According to Christine, family finances were a domestic matter, which fell into the range of her duties. Besides, her husband was too busy to handle things around the house, including family expenses. Several housewives explained that their husbands were too busy with work, so they managed finances because they had more time.

Linda was a homemaker who controlled every penny of her family budget. During our interview, Linda described a context that illustrates her absolute power over family finances:

> Finances are not an issue for us at all, but I still think we should not waste money on material goods. For example, do you see that new sofa in our living room? It's new. My husband asked to buy it for a very long time. It's very, very expensive. You would not believe how much it costs! When he asked to buy that, I said, "No, it's a waste of money." He kept trying to convince me, but I

kept saying no [laughs]. In the end, he got really angry and said: "Why can't I buy something I like? I have worked so hard for so long. I'm not twenty-something or thirty-something anymore. I am in my fifties. We don't worry about money anymore. Why can't I buy something I want?" Seeing his persistence, I finally said OK. He almost begged [laughs].

Again, a clear division of labor along the work-family line is illustrated in Linda's narrative. The wife is given responsibilities in the family domain, including family financial decisions. In fact, several second-generation young adults expressed their amazement that their mothers controlled the money although they were not the primary breadwinners. Megan, a thirty-year-old doctoral student at a prestigious university in the Chicago area, vividly described the power dynamic between her parents when it came to money in the following conversation:

GU: In your family, who is in charge of finances?

MEGAN: My mother.

GU: Do you know why?

MEGAN: I don't know [smiles]. . . . I think it's really funny [smiles]. Yes, my father is the one who brings, you know, most of the income home. But he'd give the check to my mom, and he gets allowances from her. Just recently when I was home, my Dad said he needed more money, and then my Mom said, "Well, I just gave you twenty dollars!" And then he had to itemize where he spent his money. He had to go to the gas station, and I didn't have any money for lunch, so he gave me some money. So, he had to explain where every dollar went. So, that's the arrangement.

Regardless of her dominance over family money, Megan's mother did most of the housework. Megan's father was a U.S.-trained computer engineer with a PhD. Her mother was a middle-school English teacher in Taiwan. She quit the job she loved and migrated to California when her husband secured a professional job after graduation, and she stayed at home during the early years of her family's settlement. After her children entered school, she took a couple of courses at a community college and began working part time in various business fields. Megan's parents represent a typical gendered pattern of immigration and work trajectories among the Taiwanese. They also demonstrate a typical gender division of labor among Taiwanese immigrant couples—the wife controls the money and does most of the housework.

Employed or not, many married Taiwanese immigrant women independently manage their families' budgets and financial investments. Christine, Linda, and several other housewives explained that they had more time than their husbands because they were stay-at-home moms and finances were included in their family duties. In contrast, employed women often used management abilities and skills to justify why they oversaw family economies, as the following narratives reveal:

> I am in charge of our family finances. My husband is not very good with money, and his math is not very good, either [laughs]. So, of course, it's me who makes financial decisions. There's no need to discuss with him. I just make decisions for us [laughs]. (Judy)

> I am in charge of our family finances. I am better at budgeting and managing money than my husband. He can use the money because we have a joint account, but I make major decisions for our family. He is not very good at it [laughs]. (Cindy)

> I am the one who manages family finances, because I'm more realistic than my husband. I'm a better manager than him [laughs]. So, yes, I control the money. (Lauren)

Judy's and Cindy's husbands both had PhDs, just like themselves, and both women reported that they were better at managing money than their spouses. Lauren's husband had a master's in computer science and was a computer programmer. She explained that she controlled the expenses for the well-being of the family because her husband tended to buy expensive things, and she was more conscious about saving money. These rationales are similar to those women who said they were better at cleaning, so they did most housework. Their justifications illustrate a practical logic. More important, when these women described their decision-making power over family finances, their narratives conveyed senses of pride and empowerment, what I call the *capable self*.

Among the few women who deferred family financial decisions to their husbands, time and interest were offered to explain this division of labor. As Tracy said, "My husband is in charge of our family finances because I don't have time. I work long hours and am very busy. I don't have time for that." A college professor, Jamie, explained, "I don't like to manage money. It's not my thing. I don't like to see bills [smiles], so I let my husband handle family finances. It works out well." A homemaker, Sophia, said, "My husband likes to manage money, so it's one less thing for me to worry about. I'm already too busy with the kids and housework." Although these women did not oversee family budgets themselves, they clarified that they could freely use family money without asking their husbands for permission.

About a half of dual-income couples jointly managed finances. They had joint accounts and did not clearly assign one or the other to handle money. As Sue described the situation, "We have a joint account, so aren't very clear about who is in charge of finances. My husband pays bills, and my salary is deposited directly to our account. I can use the money however I want and don't have to ask." Elena said, "We don't really assign someone to manage the money. Sometimes my husband does it, sometimes I do. We have a joint account, and we both have a checkbook. So, we both handle family money." These women shared equal power with their spouses to make financial decisions for their families. They discussed major purchases and investments, but made independent decisions on daily expenses and purchases.

Managing money is more than a form of family labor. Financial decisions, such as household budgets and stock investments, sometimes involve taking risks that could potentially threaten family survival. Who makes financial decisions for the family also speaks to power relations between the couple. In this study, regardless of their employment status, married Taiwanese immigrant women dominated or jointly made decisions concerning family finances. This phenomenon significantly differs from many previous studies of immigrant women, who gained more control over finances because of their increased contributions to the family economy.

Conclusion

Gender and immigration scholars often discuss spousal relations by examining two indicators: the gender division of domestic labor and bargaining power over family finances. Previous studies have shown that immigrant women's greater contributions to the family economy, because of their employment in the host society, enhance their status at home, thereby enabling them to negotiate a greater share of housework from their husbands and gain more decision-making power over family budgets. Meanwhile, immigrant women's exposure to Western gender ideology also increases their awareness and desire to pursue egalitarianism.[7] Nevertheless, the case of Taiwanese immigrant women complicates our understanding of the connections of work, family, culture, and power and their interactive effects on spousal relations.

While some consider Confucian gender culture the norm, most women use practical reasoning—employment status and skills—to explain why the couple divides their labor the way they do. For instance, homemakers believe that the domestic arena is their territory because they are not employed. Following this logic, everything domestic is their sole responsibility, including housework and family finances. Therefore, the women do all the housework and they control the family economy with great power. Employment status draws a clear boundary between work and family, assigning different tasks to husbands and wives accordingly. Both culture and not being employed shape a sense of *domestic self* in the women's perceptions of their roles in the family.

However, such practical reasoning does not succeed when employed women use the same logic to negotiate a greater share of housework from their husbands. Working full time, many professional women try to convince their husbands that it is only fair that the couple shares housework. Nevertheless, their husbands tend to use Confucian culture to argue that housework is women's job. In three-generation households, mothers-in-law reinforce this traditional gender ideology and demand traditional gender practice. As a result, most employed women continue to shoulder all household responsibilities. Regardless, many women who do not live with in-laws hire domestic workers and gardeners to help them with their second shift. In other words, culture is used more often by husbands and in-laws than by wives to interpret the labor division at home.

Those couples who equally divide household work begin their egalitarian practice early in their relationship and undergo few changes over time. No one cites Western culture as an influence on these behaviors. Nevertheless, these wives are aware of their deviance from Confucian gender practice and describe their husbands as unconventional or atypical Taiwanese men. These unconventional husbands face social pressure in their ethnic community, and they are sometimes mocked for lacking masculinity.

Individuals' skills, abilities, and preferences are another type of practical reasoning mentioned frequently when subjects explain who does what for the family. Some women comment that they are better than their husbands at cleaning and cooking, so they do most of the work around the house. Many women who dominate family finances also proudly claim that they are better at managing money than their husbands, what I call a *capable self* that displays a sense of competence and empowerment. Others explain that they do not like to manage money, so they entrust their husbands with financial decisions. No subject needs her spouse's permission to use money as all women have joint accounts. A few have an additional saving account only for themselves.

In *The Second Shift*, Arlie Hochschild differentiates gender ideologies from gender practices in dual-earner families. She argues that individuals' cultural ideas of their gender and marital roles do not always align with their actual gender practices, which involves instrumental actions, planning, and emotion work.[8] In the case of Taiwanese immigrant families, women's gender ideologies and practices do not always align. For instance, only a small group of women show consistency between their gender ideology (the domestic self shaped by Confucian culture) and gender practice (domestic responsibility). In contrast, many women believe that they abide by traditional gender norms in their household responsibilities; however, their dominance over family financial decisions is by no means traditional, especially for housewives (e.g., as seen in Linda's case). The women's narratives reveal various gender strategies they use to rationalize material contradictions, such as unemployment status, work-family territory, and individuals' skills. These gendered cultural narratives provide valuable information for understanding nuances in individuals' gender strategies.

In summary, the women's rationalizations of their families' division of labor and financial management paint a very different picture from what is presented in the immigration literature. Married women's economic contributions do not serve as a key factor that shapes spousal power relations in the case of Taiwanese immigrants. Rather, the gendered work-family division, Confucian gender culture, and individual skills together construct how subjects justify and negotiate their gender practice at home. Therefore, spousal relations are complex dynamics influenced by various social variables and their intertwined effects.

5
Performing Confucian Patriarchy

My mother-in-law took away my baby because he cried during
the night and my husband couldn't sleep well. I traveled to
Taiwan several times, trying to bring him back. But she did
not allow me to.... My son is almost sixteen-month-old, and
I still can't get him back. I miss him terribly [weeping].
—Amy, 30, intern psychologist

When I asked my husband to help me with housework, my
mother-in-law would be very angry. She always intervened if I
asked my husband to do dishes or if I argued with him. Every
time when I had a fight with my husband, she blamed me for
causing problems. She believed that her son was always right and
that any problem we had in the family must be my fault.
—Tiffany, 52, retired computer programmer

Everything I do is wrong in my mother-in-law's eyes. She even gave me
a list of ten major faults she found in me. It was very hurtful. I could
not stop crying when I saw the list. I am just useless and worthless
to her. At work, I make all the decisions and I am in control, but at
home, I have to be submissive. I feel so powerless and miserable.
—Jen, 50, entrepreneur

Amy, a young, married professional, began her immigrant life after
earning a master's degree in psychology and finishing an intern-
ship at a U.S. university. When her first child was born, her husband's parents visited and stayed with the couple for two months.

This was the beginning of Amy's nightmare. During the months-long visit, Amy's mother-in-law took over everything: she cooked, arranged things around the house, and took care of the newborn. Amy's mother-in-law asked her to rest in bed all the time, and she was not allowed to hold her baby. In tears, Amy described the misery she endured: "I was not allowed to get out of the bed or pump breast milk. My mother-in-law insisted that I stay in bed full time in order to rest. She said pumping breast milk is harmful for my body, so I was not allowed to do that. She fed and played with the baby and they [my husband and his parents] often gathered and laughed in the living room. I was alone in my room, crying all the time. I had to sneak out during the night when they fell asleep in order to see and hold my own baby. I was devastated and miserable." Because the newborn cried throughout the night, Amy's husband, Tom, did not sleep well and complained to his mother. At the end of the visit, Amy's mother-in-law decided to bring the baby to Taiwan, against Amy's will, so Tom could get quality sleep. Amy was devastated and helpless. She took several trips to Taiwan to try to bring her baby back to the United States. Unfortunately, each time she surrendered to her mother-in-law's authority and returned empty-handed. The baby was sixteen months old at the time of our interview, and Amy still could not get him back. She showed me a picture of her son and said in deep sadness: "I miss him. Every time I see a baby, I cannot help but cry so badly. Because it always reminds me of my baby. So I try not to look at little children. I would break down [crying]. . . . I wonder when I can finally take care of my own child [continues crying]." Shocked by her experience, I asked Amy why she had loyally obeyed her mother-in-law.

"What else can I do? She is my mother-in-law. I cannot make her unhappy," Amy said, weeping.

I will never forget her helpless, powerless, empty look—a look that I had seen numerous times when subjects described conflicts with their in-laws. Amy's story was not at all novel; it was similar to ones I heard repeatedly from the women in my study.

In fact, Amy was fully aware that she was being treated unfairly. Initially, she was unhappy about her mother-in-law's controlling behavior, and Amy insisted on her own opinions. Gradually, she was convinced that her refusal to comply with her mother-in-law's requests violated the Confucian cultural norms of filial piety.[1]

Amy's mother-in-law had first brought up the idea of bringing the baby to Taiwan early in her pregnancy. Amy thought the idea was ridiculous and asserted that she wanted to take care of her own child. However, her rejection led to Tom's resentment and jeopardized her spousal relationship:

> Tom was angry at me, and we did not talk for months during my pregnancy. I was extremely upset. I thought to myself, why did I need this marriage? We did not even talk to each other! We were supposed to support each other, but he was not supportive at all. So, one day, I said to Tom: "Why don't we get a divorce after the baby is born? Our marriage is meaningless!" He then started to explain why he was angry with me. He thought I violated the cultural value of filial piety when I turned down his mother's offer to take care of our baby for us. He strongly believed that we should listen to his parents because they have our best interests in mind, and that it's our culture to obey parents. He said that my disobedience violated our cultural morality. After our conversation, I began to think about this point and soften my attitudes about the whole thing.

Confucian principles of filial piety apparently affected Amy's considerations. When turning to her own parents for emotional support, Amy was advised that, according to Taiwanese culture, "A daughter-in-law should not question her mother-in-law." Although sympathetic to their daughter's pain, Amy's parents reinforced the traditional gender role expectations, and she felt compelled to act filially to her parents by listening to their advice. The risk to her marriage and consequent custody battle added to Amy's hesitation and ambivalence.

At a lunch gathering, Amy mentioned to fellow Taiwanese immigrant women that her mother-in-law refused to return her baby, and she indicated how much she missed her son. The women offered empathy and condemned her mother-in-law. Nevertheless, they advised Amy to remain silent and not to upset her mother-in-law. One friend said, "I'm so sorry to hear about this. But, she is your mother-in-law; you cannot disobey her and make her unhappy." Another woman said, "Look at the bright side. She is taking care of your baby so you can enjoy the freedom. That's why you're sitting here and having lunch with us!" An older lady added to the conversation: "Taiwanese mothers-in-law are all the same. Mine is not any better. What we [as daughters-in-law] could do is to be submissive and do what we can [to please them]. Try not to be bothered. There's nothing you can do [to change the power imbalance]. We all have been there."

The fellow immigrant women offered Amy social support, provided advice, and described their own mother-in-law stories. However compassionate and understanding, this group of women unanimously endorsed the social norm: married women should serve and obey their in-laws. The women's similar experiences with their mothers-in-law also normalized the mistreatment and justified the unequal statuses between the two generations of women. In spite of the evident depression and enormous sorrow that Amy experienced and displayed, no one within the coethnic circle—including her husband and parents—questioned the child-care arrangement her mother-in-law had demanded.

During our interview, I cautiously asked Amy, "Have you ever thought about taking your son back to the United States while nobody was watching?"

Without hesitation, Amy responded, "Oh, no, my mother-in-law would be very mad! I can't do that!"

She explained, "Because she is my mother-in-law, I cannot disobey her or make her unhappy." Amy appeared to believe firmly that it is culturally expected for a Taiwanese daughter-in-law to obey her mother-in-law and to endure any pain that accompanies her role.

I also asked Amy whether she had talked about this situation with her psychologist colleagues, who might be able to help her:

I have, but they [White colleagues] don't understand our culture. They were shocked by my situation and could not understand why. My professor once said to me: "Why don't you just get a divorce? Why do you have to suffer like this? You bear too much! You would not be able to be yourself and do what you want to do if you continue to do nothing about it." You see, they don't understand why I have to endure the pain and why I have to obey my mother-in-law. I have no choice. She is my mother-in-law, so I cannot make her unhappy. It's the way I was brought up. In order to maintain peace [in the family], you have to be tolerant, and you have to be filial.

Unlike her coethnics who advised tolerance, Amy's White colleagues suggested divorcing her husband, bringing the baby back against the wishes of her mother-in-law, and filing a lawsuit against her mother-in-law. Nevertheless, Amy interpreted these ideas as culturally inappropriate and continued to believe that she should not rock the boat by defying her mother-in-law. She also praised her husband's virtues of filial piety and did not wish to end her marriage. However, the enormous pain that came with her "voluntary choice" was too much to bear.

On the one hand, Amy was aware of the unfairness to her and that she was in a great deal of pain. On the other hand, she felt compelled to fulfill her culturally expected gender role. For over two years, Amy struggled with overwhelming feelings of ambivalence, depression, and loneliness from not seeing her son. Confused and shattered, Amy helplessly read her psychology textbooks daily with the hope of finding counseling techniques that could help her handle her crushing emotions of despair and powerlessness.

Amy's story may be unthinkable for many. However, women's obedience to their mothers-in-law and their consequent psychological suffering is by no means unique. Similar stories emerged repeatedly during my interviews with Taiwanese immigrant women and in my ethnographic fieldwork over the years. In fact, in-law relations are a major source of distress in Taiwanese immigrant women's lives; they are also the only domain in which these women conform consistently to the Confucian patriarchal system, despite the unbearable pain that accompanies this cultural compliance.

In this chapter, I document the prevalent in-law inequality in Taiwanese immigrant families, and I discuss how it creates enormous distress in married women's lives. I examine the role of significant others, both the women's husbands and their own mothers, in sustaining the in-law inequality and cultural value of filial piety in Confucianism. Finally, I discuss how women's senses of self are silenced by their cultural compliance, and how employed women and homemakers use different strategies to mitigate the distress that results from Confucian patriarchy.

In-Law Inequality and Married Women's Distress

Both Taiwanese immigrant men and women abide by Confucianism faithfully when interacting with the husband's parents. In my study, in-law inequality is sustained even among the most egalitarian couples. Such inequality is also an arena in which Confucian culture is manifested the most in Taiwanese American life. Women's narratives show the most consistent patterns of this manifestation when they explain their obedient behaviors and describe the unfair treatment from their mothers-in-law.

Because middle-class Taiwanese immigrant families are affluent and well settled in suburban White areas, many husbands invite their parents and relatives to visit, usually without their wives' consent. These guests often stay for a long time, ranging from two months to several years per visit, and many families live with the husbands' mothers. Three-generation cohabitation is usually initiated when the husband's father passes away, and his widowed mother moves to the United States to live with the immigrant family.

A more prevalent practice is that the husband's parents visit for several months every year or every other year. Round-trip airfare from Taiwan costs a lot of money (approximately $2,000 per person, usually paid by the immigrant family); therefore, parents-in-law tend to stay as long as their tourist visas allow (six months). In some families, the husband's siblings live with the couple while studying in the United States or exploring the possibility of immigration.

Although the wife's side of the family sometimes visits, they usually stay for only a few weeks, and they visit less frequently than the husband's relatives do because, in Taiwanese culture, a married couple's home belongs to the husband's family. Therefore, the social assumption is that the husband's relatives, especially his parents, can visit for as long and as frequently as they wish. This taken-for-granted social practice, however, creates enormous distress in married women's lives.

Hosting guests involves a lot of cooking, cleaning, shopping, and doing laundry, responsibilities that usually fall on the wife but not the husband (all of the subjects in my study reported doing their in-laws' laundry). Hosting guests for months, sometimes years, implies that the women must shoulder double or triple the regular load of housework for a nuclear family. Moreover, for married women, hosting in-laws is very different from hosting their own parents or siblings.

Michelle, a forty-one-year-old housewife, worked as a financial consultant in Taiwan before migrating to the United States. When Michelle's parents visited, she was able to sleep in because her mother got up early to cook breakfast and clean the house. After breakfast or lunch, Michelle went shopping with her parents and enjoyed their time together. In contrast, during the six months each year when her parents-in-law lived with the family, Michelle woke up early to cook breakfast and clean the house. She was always tense and stressed because her in-laws nagged constantly, followed her around the house, and demanded traditional gender roles.

Michelle had to do a lot more during her in-laws' stay and was left home alone with them when her husband, Joseph, went to work during the week. For example, instead of light cooking and occasionally getting take-out from restaurants that she and her nuclear family often enjoyed in their American life, Michelle was expected to prepare meals the "Taiwanese way" during her in-laws' stays—typically four main-course dishes, a bowl of soup, and dessert or fruit at each meal. Even on nights when Michelle had social gatherings, she had to prepare dinner for her in-laws before she left the house. Typical American food that her children loved—pizza, fried chicken, sandwiches—was not allowed when her parents-in-law were present. In other words, it was much more than just hosting; it was serving her in-laws dutifully as an obedient daughter-in-law and doing everything her in-laws demanded.

I witnessed the contrast in emotions that Michelle exhibited with and without her in-laws' presence. Every year before her in-laws' visit, Michelle stocked up on several inhalers because the stress often triggered her asthma. She often found, and sometime faked, reasons to get out of her house to avoid interactions with her in-laws. She also often complained to coethnics about various instances of mistreatment.

Michelle's mother-in-law nagged a lot about the food she cooked and how she prepared it, what her children ate and wore, and what she bought. Sometimes, Michelle was so angry that she left home and drove around town for several hours to calm down. Each year right after her in-laws left, Michelle took down the decorations that her mother-in-law had put in the house and rearranged the house in the way she liked until the next year when her in-laws returned. She also spent time with friends and dined out often when her in-laws were not living with her family. Her happiness was so obvious that everyone easily sensed her big smile from a mile away during the months when her in-laws were absent.

Because Michelle was so unhappy and her in-laws' airfare consumed a significant portion of the family's single income, I asked her whether her parents-in-law could reduce their visit frequency or duration. She responded in a gloomy tone: "It's impossible.

Joseph said it's nonnegotiable. He insisted that having his parents here every year was his duty, as a son, to fulfill the cultural virtue of filial piety." Michelle felt angry and believed it was unfair that Joseph booked his parents' flights annually despite her opposition because she was the one who had to serve them. Joseph stayed at work longer than usual when his parents visited as a way to avoid seeing the stressful interactions between his parents and his wife. His avoidance and absence resulted in Michelle's feelings of hurt, neglect, and unfairness. More than once, Michelle told me, "It's him who brings them here, but it's me who has to do all the work!"

Michelle's resentment grew year after year, and her spousal relationship deteriorated significantly because of the living arrangement. Although she complained frequently to her husband and coethnics, Michelle never said a word in front of her in-laws. She harbored her anger and did everything her in-laws demanded. On numerous occasions, Michelle told me that she hated having her in-laws there, but she had to serve them dutifully to fulfill her role as a Taiwanese daughter-in-law.

Ironically, Michelle's parents-in-law were fairly pleased with her serving them, and they praised her dutifulness to their relatives in Taiwan. One summer, Michelle travelled alone to visit her parents in Taiwan and volunteered to clean her in-laws' house for a week. I asked her why she did that because nobody asked her to. She explained: "That's what I should do [as a daughter-in-law] to show filial piety." According to Michelle, her in-laws' annual visit of six months and her submission were considered displays of filial piety by her husband, in-laws, in-laws' friends, relatives, neighbors, her own parents, and Taiwanese society in general. She explained that she could do nothing to change Taiwanese cultural expectations of daughters-in-law, and defying the norm was unthinkable and unforgiveable. As a result, Michelle continued to endure the distress year after year, despite the fact that it had significantly damaged her spousal relationship and her physical and psychological well-being.

Michelle's story suggests the symbolic capital attached to the role of filial daughters-in-law in the Taiwanese community.

However painfully and reluctantly, Michelle gained symbolic benefits from performing Confucian patriarchy. Married women's social reputations and statuses are at stake in their relations and interactions with their in-laws. Failing to fulfill their gender role expectations could bring social stigma and censure, not only to the woman but also to her parents. As a result, Confucian in-law hierarchy persists.

When I met Rachel, she was a fifty-year-old U.S.-educated professional who had worked as a computer programmer in the United States for more than two decades. During our interview, she described several instances in which she fought for fair treatment in the workplace by confronting her boss, filing a grievance against a sexist colleague, and seeking help from her union to resolve a contract issue. Nevertheless, her sense of equity and justice was limited to the work domain. When it came to family, Rachel conformed to Taiwanese cultural norms that place daughters-in-law in the lowest position of the patrilineal household. She lived with her parents-in-law and dutifully served them for thirteen years, until her divorce. Rachel recalled the context in which the decision to live with her parents-in-law was made: "In 1988, my parents-in-law moved in with us after their early retirement. I did not get a chance to say no or to negotiate the arrangement. At that time, we [had] just got married and didn't have much money. My in-laws put a down payment on a house and asked us to buy it. They said it was a gift for us. Soon after we bought the house, my husband asked me to sign my name on a card addressed to his parents, which said 'Thank you for the generous gift, and welcome to live with us.' The next thing I knew, we were living with my parents-in-law."

I asked Rachel if she had discussed the living arrangement before signing the card that her then husband had prepared:

I strongly opposed the living arrangement because I wanted my family to be my [nuclear] family, but my husband said "It's nonnegotiable." He insisted that we must live with his parents in order to fulfill the cultural morality of filial piety. He also said that his parents bought the house, so it was theirs; they surely could live with us. He even said that his parents were his gods and should be mine, too. My opposition was useless, so I painfully accepted the arrangement. I was suffering. . . . I felt oppressed in that situation. . . . no matter what I said and how miserable I felt, it was in vain. . . . The decision had been made, and I was not part of it.

Regardless of Rachel's opposition, her parents-in-law moved in as soon as the house was ready. During her thirteen years of marriage, Rachel had numerous arguments and conflicts with her mother-in-law, who dominated everything in the household. To maintain the peace, Rachel had to allow her mother-in-law to make all of the decisions, from the color of the walls, to where to put the dishes, to what furniture to buy. Every time Rachel made a household decision, her mother-in-law complained and criticized it repeatedly until she had the final say about what to do, which usually differed from Rachel's wishes.

Tired of fighting and arguing over little things, Rachel gave up and yielded the decision-making power to her mother-in-law. Extremely unhappy, she underwent psychological therapy for years to manage her depression. Rachel learned many coping mechanisms from therapy and reading self-help books; however, she continued to surrender herself to the cultural authority of her mother-in-law and did whatever she demanded. The patriarchal in-law inequality remained in the household until her divorce.

In fact, Rachel's divorce was spurred on by her mother-in-law after a violent episode in her home. One night, Rachel called the police when her husband hit her during an argument. Rachel's mother-in-law blamed her for bringing shame to the family, and she insisted that the couple get a divorce. Rachel described her heartbroken moment: "They [my parents-in-law] sat at the dining table with my husband and demanded him to divorce me. They were also talking about calling my parents and asking them to take me back to Taiwan. They were discussing my marriage without involving me or asking my opinion. I was crying in the living room by myself. It was my marriage that they were talking about, *my marriage!*"

Rachel's parents flew from Taiwan immediately after receiving a phone call from her in-laws. They apologized repeatedly and begged their in-laws to forgive Rachel. However, her in-laws insisted that nothing could amend the shame and humiliation, and they refused to "take her back." They also refused to let Rachel's parents stay in their house during the divorce process and forced them to leave. Although still hoping for a second chance for her marriage for her children's sake, Rachel complied and got a divorce as her parents-in-law commanded. Her ex-husband remarried a much younger Taiwanese woman soon after the divorce—an arranged marriage by his parents. Rachel remained single.

During our interview, Rachel painfully described how difficult it had been for her and her children to adapt over the years. For about two years, she could not sleep. Her teenage daughter once left home for a few days to show her anger, and her son's academic performance went downhill after the divorce. Rachel took a new job two hours away from where her ex-husband lived as a way to start her life over, but she struggled to ensure her children's well-being from that distance because her ex-husband had primary custody.

Beth was a forty-four-year-old U.S.-educated professional who described her anger when her mother-in-law demanded traditional gender roles. A busy professional who often skipped breakfast, Beth got up early and cooked breakfast for her mother-in-law one weekday during her visit. Not seeing bacon, which was a favorite of Beth's husband, her mother-in-law immediately yelled at her for not being a good wife. What followed was an hour-long lecture (mostly nagging) on how a Taiwanese wife should prioritize her husband's well-being over everything else, and devote herself to taking good care of her husband. Beth's mother-in-law also informed her of what she should do to serve her husband well. Beth left home quietly without saying anything that morning, as she was running late for work. However, that night, she checked into a hotel room and stayed for three days until her husband begged her to come home. She was still angry when recalling the incident: "I don't even cook breakfast for myself [or my husband]! I did it for her, and she didn't even appreciate it a bit! On what grounds did she have any reason to condemn me?! My husband can make his own breakfast and bacon. I work full time and earn more money than him. He should be making breakfast for me [laughs]! She was just being ridiculous!" However angry, Beth never confronted her mother-in-law, and she tried to avoid interactions with her by going to work early and coming home late. Harboring feelings of injustice and hurt, Beth chose avoidance disguised as acquiescence. This coping mechanism was fairly prevalent among employed subjects.

Katie, another professional, maintained silence and avoided her mother-in-law as much as possible for ten years. Her husband invited his parents and brother's family to live with the couple without consulting Katie. However, Katie had to do most of the work, hosting and serving her in-laws, including doing her brother-in-law's laundry and dirty dishes. Not happy about the living arrangement, Katie complained to her husband in private but gave in because she also believed that this arrangement was not negotiable, according to Taiwanese culture. Rather, she tried to stay late at work and volunteered for weekend work assignments to get out of her house as much as possible.

For housewives who do not work outside of the home, avoidance is almost impossible. These women are with their in-laws most of the time, even more than they are with their husbands and school-aged children. For instance, Linda, Michelle, Christine, Frances, and Gina had nowhere to go when their in-laws visited because they were homemakers. Left alone with their in-laws during the week, these housewives had a ton of work to do—cooking, cleaning, doing the laundry, and taking their in-laws places. All of their mothers-in-law nagged unreasonably and it was very stressful for the women.

Linda's mother-in-law often criticized her cooking. When the food was not cooked the way she liked, her mother-in-law would throw it away and ask Linda to recook it. On several occasions, her mother-in-law commented that Linda was useless to the family because she was unemployed. She suggested Linda work as a dishwasher at a Chinese restaurant to bring additional income to the family, although she knew her son was in a management position and had a very high income.

Moreover, Linda's mother-in-law shopped a lot during her visit and always asked Linda to pay for the expensive jewelry and skin-care products she purchased at department stores. Linda once ran around town trying to find a big diamond necklace because her mother-in-law complained that the one Linda had bought for her—a two-carat diamond in white gold—was not big enough. One summer, Linda's parents-in-laws brought along their daughters and grandchildren to visit her family, and they stayed for six weeks. Her mother-in-law told the additional guests to buy anything they wanted because "Linda will pay for them."

Linda and her husband were also responsible for all expenses during her in-laws' visits, including their tours to other cities in the United States and their round-trip tickets from Taiwan. Linda was unhappy about the enormous amount of money they spent on her in-laws, but never once turned down her mother-in-law's requests. She explained: "She is my mother-in-law, my husband's mother. I cannot disobey her. It's our culture. I try to do everything she asks in order to make her happy. She is very mean to me and often says nasty things to me. But my husband is very good to me, and our relationship is solid. I cannot defy his mother, because I would put him in a difficult position. I don't want to jeopardize my marriage because of her."

Like Linda, when considering how to interact with their in-laws, many women weighed the potential influence of these relationships on their marriages. For instance, Nicole, a retired computer programmer, dutifully served her mother-in-law for more than ten years. Her mother-in-law moved in with the family in suburban Chicago after Nicole's father-in-law died. During those years, Nicole's mother-in-law helped with housework, especially cooking, because both Nicole and her husband worked full time. Although she disliked her mother-in-law's cooking, Nicole always praised her at the dinner table. However, she snuck out from time to time to a good restaurant to compensate herself for tolerating her mother-in-law's cooking. When her mother-in-law struggled with Alzheimer's during her final years, Nicole insisted on not hiring any help. She fed and bathed her mother-in-law by herself, as she perceived it as her duty as a daughter-in-law to do so. She said: "I did not hire help during my mother-in-law's last years, nor did I send her to a nursing home. It's not our culture, so I didn't want to do that. I took care of her every day, including feeding her, bathing her, and cleaning up her poop. I also came home during my lunch break to check on her. It's what I should do as a daughter-in-law. Although she never said 'Thank you,' I could sense that she was very appreciative. My husband was touched by what I did for his mother—I did much more than him for his mother—and it strengthened our relationship."

Like Nicole, several women in the study not only took care of their husbands' parents but also considered serving their parents-in-law as their responsibility. In these households, the husbands usually appreciated what their wives did, which strengthened their spousal relationships. *Emotional economies* are at play in these family dynamics: mothers-in-law feel entitled to their privilege and power, wives feel obligated to serve their in-laws, and husbands feel indebted to their wives' dutiful service as filial daughters-in-law. These emotions of entitlement, obligation, and gratitude are displayed and exchanged, which complicates the power dynamics both overtly and indirectly.[2]

However, regardless of the subjects' subservient behaviors and efforts to please their in-laws, not all in-laws appreciated what the women did for their families. For instance, Jen's and Christine's mothers-in-law were unhappy about their performances as mothers and wives, and gave them lists of "ten major faults." Interestingly, the two lists were quite similar. Examples of these faults included "You should let the kids eat dinner before doing homework," "You iron your husband's shirts incorrectly," "Your cooking sucks," "You should not argue with your husband," and "You talk too much with your friends." Both Jen and Christine were very upset when they received these lists. Jen commented: "Everything I do is wrong in my mother-in-law's eyes. She even gave me a list of ten major faults she found in me. It was very hurtful. I could not stop crying when I saw the list. I am just useless and worthless to her. At work, I make all the decisions and I am in control, but at home, I have to be submissive. I feel so powerless and miserable."

A business owner, Jen handled millions of dollars in revenue each year. She was not at all afraid of the challenges and disadvantages of being an Asian woman when competing with men or with White-owned companies in mainstream U.S. society. During our interview, Jen shared many experiences of her asserting autonomy toward her employees at work and overcoming stereotypes of Asian women in the business world. At home, on the contrary, she conformed to the cultural expectations of a Taiwanese daughter-in-law and acted submissively when interacting with her mother-in-law. Sadly, Jen's obedience did not earn more respect or appreciation from her mother-in-law who continued criticizing her daily in spite of Jen's efforts to please her.

When Jen's husband had an affair, her mother-in-law blamed her for not being able to keep her husband loyal. When Jen considered a divorce after she discovered the affair, her mother-in-law insisted that she stay in her marriage because, according to her mother-in-law whose husband also had cheated, "It's common for men to have affairs." Jen listened to her mother-in-law and changed her mind about filing for divorce. Feeling hurt, betrayed, and miserable for years, Jen devoted herself to work and found satisfaction and a sense of control in the workplace. She explained that she could not defy her mother-in-law or make her unhappy because it would be culturally inappropriate.

In fact, cultural appropriateness emerged as a primary explanation in the subjects' narratives when they considered how they needed to interact with their in-laws. Without exception, the women used Confucian gender norms to explain their submissive behaviors during in-law interactions, even though many struggled with the consequences of their cultural compliance.[3] Confucian beliefs of in-law status framed these women's perceptions of who they were in relation to their mothers-in-law, thereby guiding their behaviors and interactions.

The Role of Significant Others

Husbands' attitudes and actions are important factors in mediating mother- and daughter-in-law conflicts.[4] In my study, five husbands took action to reconcile the clashes between their wives and mothers. Three took their mothers out-of-town during their visits to lessen the interactions between the two women. Another man defended his wife when his mother said mean things to her. The fifth husband asked his mother, who lived with the family, not to interfere with his wife's parenting authority by promising her total control in the kitchen. These households were able to maintain peace, although the mothers-in-law did not stop distressing their daughters-in-law or making unreasonable demands. The wives in these families appreciated their husbands' actions and tolerated their in-laws more willingly than those women whose husbands did nothing constructive to support them.

In most cases, husbands supported their wives in private but never said anything to their mothers about how their wives felt, nor did they try to change their mothers' behaviors. Many husbands felt compelled to behave like chauvinists in front of their mothers to show their masculinity. Mindy described her husband's behavior: "My husband usually did dishes after dinner. But when his mother was present, he would just sit there and watch TV. He wanted to show his mother that he was a 'macho man' [smiles]! In fact, he was very egalitarian and I was the one who made important decisions for our family. But he did not want his mom to know that [I was in charge]. I just went along when he needed to show that he was the man in the house [laughs]!" In other words, even when husbands hold egalitarian ideologies and are supportive of their wives, they know they have to act a certain way to please their mothers. Using Goffman's dramaturgical perspective, this patriarchal act is a strategic performance—what I call the performance of *situational patriarchy*.[5] It is a staged gender performance based on the Confucian cultural script. Growing up in Taiwan, both men and women have internalized the social structures of gender and in-law hierarchies. They understand what the older generation expects them to do, no matter how they actually feel about the cultural expectations and what they do back stage.

Usually, gender role expectations are directly commanded in three-generation households, and any cultural violation could cause tensions, conflicts, and arguments. Tiffany described how men doing housework was taboo in her home: "Whenever I asked my husband to help me with housework, my mother-in-law would be very angry. She always intervened if I asked my husband to do dishes or if I argued with him. Every time when I had a fight with my husband, she blamed me for causing problems. She believed that her son was always right and that any problem we had in the family must be my fault." Although unhappy about her mother-in-law's biased attitudes and invalid accusations, Tiffany never argued with her, nor did she explain anything to her mother-in-law. She remained silent and asked her husband not to defy his mother. "It would be culturally inappropriate for children to question their parents, or for daughters-in-law to challenge their mothers-in-law," Tiffany explained. In fact, most women in this study believed it would be culturally inappropriate for their husbands to confront their mothers because it would violate the Confucian teaching of filial piety. In other words, many couples shared the tendency of tolerance.

Several husbands avoided interacting with their mothers by going to work early and coming home late as they tried to escape their mothers' complaints and seeing their wives in misery. Meanwhile, the women often weighed the potential effect on their marriages if they challenged their mothers-in-law. This factor complicated the women's considerations when interacting with their in-laws. Gina explained: "She is my husband's mother. I can't challenge her or make her unhappy. When she was mean to me, I just pretended that I didn't hear her or I didn't know what was going on. Whatever she said or did, I did not let it sink in. My husband is a very good guy and a good father. I cannot defy his mother and let it affect our relationship. It's my marriage that I care about, honestly. So, I just keep quiet and act submissively. As long as she is happy, everything will be okay."

Concerns about risking their spousal relationships were common among subjects, and many were willing to tolerate their mothers-in-law to protect their marriages. In contrast, many spousal relationships were damaged significantly because of husbands' unsupportive attitudes toward in-law conflicts. Tiffany described the hurt and bitterness she harbored:

> For several years, I was deeply hurt. Every time I complained about my mother-in-law, my husband got angry and defended his mother. He said that the in-law problem was only in my head because his mother never complained about living with us. I felt that I was not his priority, and that my well-being was not his concern. He enjoyed being a baby in front of his mother and was insensitive to my feelings. He had no idea how devastated I was. I was deeply disappointed and hurt. I did not feel loved and I did not think I still loved him. . . . For a long time, I could not have intimacy with my husband. . . . because he looks like his mother, and I just couldn't feel intimate when I looked at him. I thought about divorce a million times, but I did not want to lose my children. I have a good job and I am financially independent, so I would be fine. But, I did not want my children to grow up in a broken family. So, I went to a psychologist for help.

Like Tiffany, having their children's well-being in mind, most women did not seek divorce as a solution to their in-law conflicts. Moreover, because their mothers-in-law were usually much older than they were, many women considered the age factor and hesitated to violate the social norm of respecting the elderly in Confucian culture by defying their mothers-in-law. When subjects explained why they did not confront their in-laws in the case of mistreatment or unreasonable requests, they often said: "She is old. In our culture, we don't challenge the elderly"; "She will not live forever, so there's no need to make her unhappy"; and "Old people do not change, so it'd be in vain trying to change them."

Mothers were another significant other who affected these women's perceptions and behaviors. Without exception, every woman's mother advised her daughter to abide by Confucian cultural norms (i.e., obey her mother-in-law). According to the subjects, their mothers always cited cultural appropriateness when giving them advice, although they were sympathetic about the pain their daughters endured. A few mentioned to their daughters that their own mothers-in-law were much worse; therefore, "Everything will be okay eventually," as Frances recalled. "My mom said that my mother-in-law is old, so there is no need to argue with her and make her unhappy. She also reminded me that defying my mother-in-law would damage my marriage, so the best way is to tolerate the old lady and behave submissively. She will not live forever, and everything will be OK in the end. The most important thing is my marriage."

During my fieldwork, I witnessed strong support of Confucian gender norms from one immigrant woman's mother at a holiday party held by Michelle, a forty-one-year-old housewife. Michelle's mother visited from Taiwan around that time, and she cooked many traditional Taiwanese dishes for the party. As I welcomed Michelle's mother and made casual conversation with her, I unintentionally mentioned that Michelle looked very happy that day, unlike when her mother-in-law visited. Michelle's mother told me, "That is not right. She should not be like this. I need to have a conversation with her." I later mentioned this conversation to Michelle. She responded that her mother always said the same thing to her and condemned her for not being happy during her mother-in-law's visits. "But that's how I truly feel, I can't help it," said Michelle.

Similarly, other women's mothers reinforced traditional gender norms concerning in-law status. Their attitudes not only supported in-law inequality but also normalized the daughter-in-law's suffering. Surrounded by their ethnic community where filial piety is considered valuable morality and obeying the mother-in-law is perceived as a virtue of femininity, the women continued to conform to Confucian cultural expectations of womanhood and suppress their psychological suffering that resulted from their cultural compliance.

For housewives who did not have independent incomes, the potential custody battles and loss of financial support were serious matters to consider. For example, for years, Christine was angry with her mother-in-law who criticized everything she did and rarely looked her in the eye. Her husband was offensive about Christine's resentment toward his mother and blamed Christine for making his mother unhappy. At one point, Christine felt extremely disappointed and hopeless about her marriage and considered filing for divorce. However, she did not want to handle the financial risks and custody battle. Christine described her hesitation when she imagined what would happen if she divorced her husband:

> I thought about divorce, seriously. But then, I thought about the custody battle. It would kill me if I lost my kids. I stopped taking my depression medication because I did not want this to become a factor if someday I have to fight for my children's custody. My depression record could possibly be used against me. I also thought about what I would do to support myself if that day [divorce] really comes. I could probably find a job at a Chinese restaurant, washing dishes, or I could work as a maid, cleaning people's houses. But then it would not be a good situation for my kids. Right now, we are living a luxury life. We don't have to pay mortgage and we take family vacations very often. And I am in charge of our family finances and investment decisions. We have a good life here. So, I just need to learn how to cope with it.

As revealed in Christine's response, fighting custody battles and losing financial resources in a foreign country involve great risks. Her parents-in-law purchased the house in her husband's name, so she did not have any property. Although she had a joint account with her husband, Paul, most of the couple's money was invested in stocks that were in Paul's name. Therefore, getting a divorce would put Christine in a financially vulnerable position. Like the H-4 visa status, the financial risk immigrant housewives face poses a very real structural factor for them to comply with traditional gender norms—both when they give up their own sources of income at the time of immigration and when they consider ending unhappy marriages.

Christine's narrative also shows her *imagined self*, which I discuss in chapter 3. Although receiving an MBA from a U.S. university, Christine changed her plans to return and became an immigrant housewife when Paul decided to permanently settle in the United States. For more than a decade, Christine centered her life around her family. Taking care of three young children and shouldering all the housework consumed most of her time and energy. Her English became rusty, and what she learned in graduate school may no longer have been applicable in the business world. The jobs that Christine imagined herself doing were she to get a divorce—washing dishes and cleaning houses— were far from compatible with her education and family socio- economic status. Although only hypothetical, this imaginary illus- trates the influence housewifelization could produce on one's sense of self.

Silencing the Self in Cultural Compliance

The following excerpt from my interview with Marge represents the prevalent sentiment among middle-class Taiwanese immigrant women about their in-law dynamics:

> I lost my voice and visibility during her [mother-in-law's] stay. She cooked, cleaned, and reorganized my kitchen. I went to work early and stayed in my office until midnight, and then I just locked myself in my bedroom when I went home. I did not even feel like seeing my kids! If I didn't hide myself, I would be con- demned for everything I did because whatever I did was wrong in her eyes. I did not want to defy her or make her unhappy, so I

chose to silence myself. . . . Sometimes I felt I wanted to. . . . just take my kids and leave, you know. . . . it was very painful, and I was so helpless. . . . But there's nothing I can do. . . . She is my mother-in-law, so I have to accept it [the situation].

This sense of suffering reveals the deep, unshakable Confucian beliefs about in-law status in the women's cognition and the influence of these beliefs on their choice to silence themselves. Repeatedly, subjects reported: "I have no choice but to obey my mother-in-law," "I chose to remain silent in order to make her happy," and "What other choices do I have?" However, the women's choice to comply with Confucian cultural norms came at a high cost—the women's own mental health. For example, Amy was deeply depressed for two years. Rachel was in therapy for years. Beth moved into a hotel room for several days. Michelle drove around town for hours to calm down. Christine could not stop crying every time she recollected her mother-in-law's mistreatment. Frances and Linda often complained about their mothers-in-law to other immigrant women. Yet, these married women were always quiet in the presence of their in-laws, suppressing their negative emotions and true senses of self.

As I explain in chapter 2, the choices women make are constructed and constrained by social structures; their choices are often weighted by emotion-laden experiences and a hierarchy of beliefs and values. In most cases, Taiwanese immigrant women's mothers-in-law are less educated, less wealthy, and far less acculturated. Their higher status in the family hierarchy than their daughters-in-law is socially constructed by Confucian cultural beliefs. Socialized in this ethnic gender system, daughters-in-law tend to accept their lower status and behave submissively. Were they to defy the in-law hierarchy, they would face potential spousal conflicts, disturbance of relational harmony in the three-generation household, and censure from their ethnic community—even from their own mothers. Their social reputation is also at stake. In the private space of the family, no competing gender ideologies exist to offer alternatives. Therefore, accepting the status quo becomes the only option. By silencing themselves, subjects acquiesce to Taiwanese in-law inequality and reproduce the patriarchal social structure as defined by Confucianism.

Because the patriarchal nature of Confucian in-law inequality contradicts the values of individual autonomy and relational equity that these women learned in the United States, they experience overwhelming emotions in deliberating their choices. Although voluntary, their submissive behavior is a depressing and painful choice constrained by Confucian social norms. They engage in what Hochschild calls *emotion work* when suppressing their true feelings and acting obediently in their roles as filial daughters-in-law.[6] As a result, relational harmony is achieved, and Confucian social order is reproduced and sustained.

Nevertheless, these women are by no means victims of Confucian norms. As I explain in chapter 2, social structure both constrains and enables, and that power imposition always generates resistance. However agitated they feel, the women manage to mitigate the distress that results from their cultural conformity. On the surface, women's cultural compliance reproduces inequality; however, the varied forms of resisting power should be highlighted and considered a means to exert agency. For instance, employed subjects use avoidance as a disguise of acquiescence, and some seek counseling services provided by their companies or private practitioners. Housewives often find reasons to get out of their homes to avoid interacting with their in-laws; they also frequently complain to coethnic women, who understand their culture, in-law issues, and struggles. Below, I illustrate the contexts of these resistance strategies.

EMPLOYED WOMEN: WORKPLACE ESCAPE AND COUNSELING

Avoidance was a fairly prevalent behavior among the subjects, especially those who were employed. For example, Katie, Sue, Jamie, and many others stayed at the office as long as they could and volunteered for weekend business trips to avoid interactions with their mothers-in-laws. These women gave their home spaces to their mothers-in-law and used work to occupy their minds. Many found peace away from the home, but also felt sad about their invisibility and lost space in their own homes. For example, Beth volunteered to take a weeklong work-related trip during her mother-in-law's monthlong visit. She explained why she needed the trip:

I just had to get out of my house. I was going crazy. She criticized everything and changed everything around in the house. I was very irritated and couldn't rest in my own home. She also had different opinions about my son's after-school activities and complained that he did not speak Mandarin well. Everything was wrong when she was here, and I felt I couldn't breathe. . . . When I was talking to other Taiwanese women about this situation, they envied me that my mother-in-law stayed with us *only* for a month! *Only a month*? Are you kidding me? Every day when she was here, it felt like forever! I was dying inside!

Like Beth, many employed women used their workplaces as escapes from their mothers-in-law. Work was an easy disguise for employed women when avoiding in-law interactions, although they lost their own spaces at home. A few returned to their homes at the end of the day only to shoulder more housework. As Katie described her situation:

I stayed at my office or in the library as late as I could. In addition to my parents-in-law, my brothers-in-law's families were living with us. For ten years, there were eighteen people living in my house. It was very noisy all the time, and I couldn't work or study for my graduate degree. I was suffering. . . . I didn't know how I survived those years. I had to cook dinner after work and then went back to my office to work or went to the library to study. When I came home around midnight, there were dishes in the sink and tons of dirty laundry waiting. They were guests, so I couldn't ask them to do housework. Although they helped out here and there, I felt that housework was my obligation because it's my home, not theirs. I was exhausted all the time and became very sick.

Both Beth's and Katie's narratives reveal the ambivalent and conflicting emotions that many subjects shared. On the one hand, the women were aware of their unhappiness and its cause. They suffered from their vulnerable positions and tried to escape from their in-laws. On the other hand, they were aware of Confucian gender norms, which expect them to serve their in-laws dutifully and endure any pain that accompanies this role. Confucian gender culture powerfully constrains women's perceptions of their in-laws' status and behaviors. Regardless of their evident suffering, none of the women ever confronted their in-laws and expressed how they truly felt. As a result, the workplace became a shelter that provided a temporary escape.

Some professionals used counseling services offered by their corporations or private practitioners to help mitigate their distress that resulted from in-law inequality. As mentioned earlier, Rachel sought psychological therapy to help mitigate her depression that resulted from her in-law conflicts. Initially, Rachel's husband went with her to show support, but refused to continue going after a few sessions. He could not stand how Rachel talked about his parents. He told Rachel, "You are mentally ill, so you should continue therapy and learn how to change yourself. But I don't want to hear you attacking my parents." According to Rachel, her mother-in-law was happy she was seeing a therapist, as she explained, "She said that I was the one who had [psychological] problems, not her, and that it was me who needed to change, not her." Rachel stayed in therapy for almost two years and read many self-help books. During therapy sessions, Rachel was able to say what was on her mind and express her true emotions. Nevertheless, she found the help of therapy limited: "Americans [Whites] don't understand our culture. My therapist asked why I had to live with my parents-in-law and why I didn't just ask them to move out. This is so ridiculous! They [Whites] don't understand that it's not even an option for me [in our culture]! They just don't get it! The therapy was not helpful because my therapist couldn't really understand why it was so difficult for me and why I could not disobey my mother-in-law."

Most subjects who sought counseling services to help deal with their in-law issues shared this cultural barrier. For instance, Tracy described similar frustrations with her White therapist: "They [Whites] don't understand our culture. I was in therapy for a while, but stopped going because it didn't help at all. I told my therapist that I had mental breakdowns because my in-laws had lived with us for six months, and I was totally stressed out. She asked why I didn't just ask them to leave to solve the problem. You see? There was such a huge cultural gap! Are you kidding me? I would not need your help if I could [laughs]! They just don't understand our culture. They don't understand why I can't ask them to leave. It's not that easy, but they don't get it!"

Regardless of this prevalent cultural barrier, the women found counseling therapeutic because it offered a safe place for them to express emotions without worrying about potential circulation of gossip, a concern they would have if they talked with fellow immigrant women. When using counseling services, the subjects usually had to explain their cultural traditions and social norms in detail in order to help their therapists understand the context of their dilemmas. Although many women complained about their therapists' lack of cultural understanding, a few found counseling helpful. As Jamie explained: "My [White] psychologist confirmed to me that I was treated as an object by my mother-in-law. I needed to hear that, so I knew it was not just my own imagination as my husband said. I needed to hear from someone else that I was seen as a baby machine by my in-laws and that the mistreatment was unfair to me! I told my therapist I wanted a divorce, but she reminded me that whom I actually wanted to divorce was my mother-in-law, not my husband. It [therapy] helped me to think through the situation and detangle my complex emotions to some extent." Using the workplace and counseling, employed women were able to avoid in-law interactions, release their emotions, and find peace in some ways.

While employed women can easily use their workplaces to escape from in-law interactions and duties, housewives are stuck with their in-laws at home. Because of their unemployed status, homemakers usually spend more time with their in-laws than with their husbands and school-age children. Avoidance is almost impossible in these families, and women experience significant distress when spending long hours with their mothers-in-law on a daily basis. For instance, Michelle's and Linda's mothers-in-law nagged constantly and often made unreasonable demands. Michelle's mother-in-law followed her everywhere in the house and criticized everything she did. Linda's mother-in-law often asked her to cook something and later wanted something else. Because their mothers-in-law did not understand English at all and did not drive, the women had to take care of everything. As a result, the workload was much more than that of their nuclear families, and the nagging and unreasonable requests only made the burden worse.

From time to time, Michelle would leave home and drive around town for several hours to calm down when she was fed up with her mother-in-law's nagging and abusive words. She also made up reasons to go out alone to avoid interacting with her in-laws. Similarly, other housewives often found various reasons to get out of their homes when they "craved for fresh air." Fellow immigrant women usually understood the situation and offered each other companionship. They went out to lunch or went shopping together whenever someone needed to escape from her in-laws.

In fact, coethnics were an important source of social support for housewives. At monthly gatherings with other immigrant mothers, the women often described the mistreatment they received from their mothers-in-law. Other women listened, commented, and provided support. Many shared similar stories about their in-law relations and expressed the same feelings of powerlessness and injustice. Complaining about their mothers-in-law and finding people who actually understood the unspeakable pain brought a sense of comfort.

At the women's social gatherings, in-law stories served as entertainment as the women humorously competed with others to find the "meanest mother-in-law" in the stories they told. However, although the group of women condemned mothers-in-law and showed great empathy toward each other, in the end they unanimously concluded that acting submissively was the only solution to the situation. The unshakable Confucian cultural beliefs of in-law status were eventually reinforced in the coethnic circle.

Conclusion

In-law dynamics in middle-class Taiwanese immigrant families illustrate the persistent inequality between two generations of women and warn of its negative effects on psychological well-being. Married women across age, occupation, and year of immigration show strikingly similar patterns of submissive behavior when interacting with their in-laws. These women draw from Confucian cultural beliefs to explain their obedient behaviors and their reluctance to transgress the social norms of their ethnic gender roles. Nevertheless, the women's cultural compliance generates overwhelming distress, as it requires them to conceal their true feelings and senses of self. In the end, performing Confucian patriarchy consumes enormous energy and emotion work.

What can explain the persistence of in-law inequality in Taiwanese immigrant families? Why do changes due to women's immigration and labor force participation not influence the patriarchal structure of in-law relations? Based on the women's narratives, I argue that Confucian culture serves as a governing social force in preserving in-law inequality in Taiwanese immigrant households. However, the perpetuation of such cultural dominance on married women's compliance is made possible by several intertwined structural and social-psychological factors.

First, international migration excuses Taiwanese couples from gratifying filial piety because all subjects immigrated initially without their parents-in-law. For sons, moving far away from their elderly parents creates a sense of guilt because they are culturally expected to care for their aging parents. Therefore, when their parents move in or visit from Taiwan, these sons are compelled to fulfill their obligations as filial children.

Second, social class plays a role in the living arrangements of three-generation households. Middle-class Taiwanese are able to host guests because most of them own spacious houses in suburban White areas. In my previous study, Taiwanese laborers did not report in-law conflicts because they did not have enough space to host relatives in their small apartments or to pay the airfares for their parents or siblings to visit.[7] Having one or more empty guest rooms at home but asking your parents to stay in a hotel is not only culturally inappropriate, it could also incur social stigma and would be too costly were immigrant couples to pay for a hotel room for months.

Third, in a Taiwanese family, gender and age intersect to construct the social structure of, and status hierarchies within, three-generation households. In addition to gender role expectations, age-based social statuses stratify the household and define behavioral norms. As I explain in chapter 2, Confucian teaching cultivates in the younger generation an imperative to always respect, honor, and obey their elders. Parents-in-law being older than the wife creates another layer of status hierarchy. Moreover, when all family members are from the same racial/ethnic group and society of origin, no contesting ethnic cultures exist to offer alternative social norms. Family as a private domestic sphere also leaves little room for competing gender ideologies, in contrast to the public sphere where gender equality is at least paid lip service. It is also more difficult to contest injustice or mistreatment in a private space than in a public domain.

For instance, in the two interracial families in my previous study, the women who married Whites used American culture to explain their labor division at home.[8] Their White husbands did much of the housework because "it's their culture," as the women said in our interviews, referring to such equality as a contrast to Taiwanese patriarchal gender norms. They also kept a distance from their in-laws, whose visits lasted only a few days with a maximum of one week. Both women called their parents-in-law by first name, a phenomenon that never occurred in one-race/ethnicity Taiwanese families I had observed over the past decade, as it is considered disrespectful in Confucian culture. Taiwanese daughters-in-law always respectfully address their Taiwanese mothers-in-law by "mom." Furthermore, many subjects behave submissively in in-law relations but act confrontationally when dealing with racial prejudice in the workplace and the larger society (see chapter 6). The contrast of their behaviors suggests that place (public vs. private spheres) matters. As I explain in chapter 2, place shapes individuals' subjectivities and their understanding of behaviors, social relations, and surroundings.

Finally, serving in-laws not only helps the women earn symbolic capital; it also strengthens their spousal relationships because they act as their husbands' deputies in accomplishing patrilineal filial piety. The relational harmony that Confucian culture highly values can be maintained without disturbance when wives suppress their negative emotions toward in-laws. These gains make the women's emotional struggles seem less significant, thereby shaping the women's willingness to endure the pain. The women's social reputations and marriages would be at stake if they chose to challenge in-law inequality. In other words, the women often weigh various pros and cons of the situation when considering what to do in their in-law interactions. In Taiwanese in-law relations, most married women consider the gains of their submission to be greater than their struggles and, thus, choose to perform Confucian patriarchy as a gender strategy. As a result, in-law inequality is sustained in three-generation households.

In *Framed by Gender*, Cecilia Ridgeway argues that gender is a primary framework for defining the self and others; it is an organizational force that shapes how individuals behave by considering themselves in relation to others. Central to this theory is the importance of hegemonic cultural beliefs about gender in shaping behaviors and organizing social relations. These beliefs also affect how individuals define themselves and others, which frame the basis for acting in social relational contexts. In modern times, cultural presumptions about gender continue to privilege men, while they position women at a lower level of respect, social esteem, and honor. Gender as a status characteristic is a significant organizing principle of behaviors and social practices that can answer why gender inequality persists in contemporary American society.[9]

Building on Ridgeway's theory, I argue that Confucian cultural beliefs about in-law status shape married Taiwanese immigrant women's perceptions of who they are in relation to their in-laws and guide their interactions. However, it does not mean that a straightforward enculturation takes place in in-law relations without questioning, defiance, or struggle. Rather, subjects' stories provide numerous instances of negotiation, resistance, contestation, adjustment, and conflict. The dominance of Confucian cultural beliefs and the persistence of in-law inequality require the presence of several intertwined structural and social-psychological factors (immigration, social class, race/ethnicity, gender, age, place, symbolic capital, emotion work, and emotional economies) that interact to reproduce and maintain the status disparity between two generations of women in Taiwanese immigrant households.

Because the patriarchal nature of in-law relations contradicts the values of individual autonomy and relational equity, women's cultural conformity is accomplished by silencing themselves at the cost of compromised mental health. In their painful conformity to the designated in-law hierarchy, the women use available resources to create varied mechanisms to cope with in-law stress and its subsequent tensions in a marriage. They find several avenues to mitigate their distress, including seeing a counselor, taking out-of-town business trips, complaining to fellow immigrant women, and making excuses to escape from home. These strategies must be recognized and considered as different forms of agency. Under in-law inequality, women's efforts to empower themselves never stop.

6

Fighting for Dignity
and Respect

In daily life, very often, people tend to assume that I can't speak
English and that I am uneducated. In fact, I have a PhD from
an Ivy League [college] and speak four languages fluently.
—Ann, 41, scientist

They [Whites] just pretend that they don't understand you. Well,
when I cursed him in English, he understood me perfectly!
—Wendy, 54, computer programmer

There were a few [White] mothers at my children's school who were very
rude. When I said "Hi," they always turned their heads and pretended that
they didn't see me. After a few times, I just stopped saying "Hi" to them.
—Linda, 53, housewife

Growing up in a patriarchal society, America was always my
dream country because it places high value on equality and
autonomy. I woke up from this dream a few years ago, when I
encountered a racist sexist colleague. I began to see the reality.
—Jamie, 43, college professor

At age thirty-two, Wendy started an entry-level job at an information technology company after working part time illegally before
acquiring her permanent residency. Migrating as a dependent,
Wendy gave up her highly respected teaching job in Taiwan and

moved to Chicago with her husband. Excited to work full time again, she did not care that her new job was in a different field and that it paid very little. She worked hard and felt enthusiastic about learning new things. After a few months, however, Wendy realized that her supervisor, a high-school graduate and White male, assigned her only trivial tasks and did not teach her what she was supposed to learn to secure her job. She confronted her supervisor, Gary, and asked why he did not give her more challenging work. Gary responded: "Well, if you know how to do my job, what am I going to do?" He continued to ignore Wendy's request to learn her job.

Frustrated by the fruitless communication with Gary, Wendy went to the manager (a White man) and revealed what had happened. She reported that Gary refused to teach her anything and asked the manager to train her so she could do her job well. Wendy's manager spent a weekend teaching her how to run a computer at which point he also discovered her intelligence and diligence. Later, the manager condemned Gary's misconduct and praised Wendy's abilities. Gary became very angry and filed a complaint to several managers about Wendy's poor English.

The company's vice president, a German immigrant man, became involved and investigated this case directly. After a thorough investigation, the vice president concluded that Wendy had done nothing wrong. He reminded all managers how to handle cases like this properly, and transferred Gary to a different department. Wendy appeared proud when recalling this incident: "They [Whites] often pretend that they don't understand you. Well, when I cursed him [Gary] in English, he understood me perfectly [smiles]! I was not afraid of him because I knew I was right, so I had nothing to be afraid of. In the United States, you need to speak up. Our [Confucian] culture teaches us to tolerate [unfair treatment], but it doesn't work here! You've got to speak up and stand up for yourself."

I asked Wendy if she worried about losing her job by going to her manager. She replied: "If I lost my job because I stood up for what was right, so be it! I'd just find another job and move on. The company is a large IT [information technology] firm. They can't just fire people without good reasons. I knew I was right, so I didn't worry about it. This is America. You cannot treat me unfairly!"

Wendy added that she had done many different jobs since arriving in the United States—jobs for which she had no background but had to take because of the restrictions of her dependent visa status and lack of fluency in English.[1] Changing jobs was not an issue for her: "What do I have to lose [for speaking up]? My job? I have done all kinds of jobs that I had no training for and have done them exceptionally well. I can also stay home. My family doesn't need my income. I work because I'm bored at home. My husband would be very happy if I become a homemaker."

As revealed in Wendy's narrative, the work trajectories of highly skilled immigrant women affect how they perceive employment and the risks of challenging unfair treatment. As documented in chapter 3, most subjects work in professions that differ from their college training because they migrated as dependents when their husbands decided to settle in the United States. Unprepared to work in the United States, many women choose in-demand jobs such as computer programming and accounting rather than jobs in their areas of interest. As a result, many perceive their jobs in the United States as "a job that brings income" rather than "a career that fulfills ambition and self-worth," as Wendy commented. These women also change jobs more frequently than their male counterparts, and they retreat to the family when necessary. While many of these women choose to work outside of the home because they do not find homemaking fulfilling, they continue to prioritize family over work.

The exposure of Taiwanese immigrant women to Western egalitarian ideologies also facilitates their sense of self-worth and independence in American society. They exhibit this newly gained autonomy in the workplace, and in their confrontational approach to work-related problems.[2] More significantly, Taiwanese immigrant women quickly adopt an American identity to frame their status beliefs when challenging unfair treatment in the workplace. While they recognize their perceived status by Whites as Asian

immigrant women, they act fearlessly based on their own perceived status as American citizens, who are entitled to equal rights
regardless of race, gender, or immigrant status.[3] In other words,
being American highlights the salience of these women's social
identities in relation to Whites. As such, this perception shapes
these women's senses of justice and affects their behaviors.

Similar to Wendy's story, workplace confrontation is surpris-
ingly common among women subjects in my study. When encountering unfair treatment, many women, including those positioned
at the lower end of the corporate ladder, stand up for themselves
and fight for justice. This phenomenon not only contradicts social
stereotypes of Asian women—submissive, quiet, and willing to
tolerate poor working conditions—but also provides an interesting
contrast to their male counterparts, who tend to normalize racial
inequality and accept the status quo in the workplace.[4]

Many homemakers reported similar confrontations when they
experienced everyday racism in U.S. society. Although lacking
fluency in English, these immigrant housewives often spoke up
when they encountered prejudiced treatment. In this chapter, I
document various contexts in which Taiwanese immigrant women
encounter prejudice and unfair treatment in their workplaces. I
also discuss how professional women and homemakers deal with
everyday racism in their lives.

Workplace Racism and Sexism

The question, "Have you ever received unfair treatment at work
because of your race or gender?" elicited numerous stories from
women about mistreatment in the workplace and the confrontations that followed. For instance, Molly, a fifty-year-old bank teller,
confronted her manager about a reduction in her salary during a
restructuring period. She recalled: "A year ago, our bank was making some restructuring adjustments, and they reduced my salary
without telling me why. I went to my manager and asked why the
bank lowered my salary. He did not expect my bold question and
couldn't explain why. So, I told him, you cannot just cut my salary

without a good reason. I work hard and do my job well. I deserve my full salary. After the meeting, they adjusted my salary back [smiles]."

Sue, a fifty-six-year-old technician in the pharmacy department at a prestigious hospital, also fought for pay equity. She recalled how she felt when she learned her salary was lower than other colleagues in the same position: "After working in the pharmacy for six years, I realized that my salary was lower than others, even than new hires. I was very angry. I worked harder than anyone else in my department. You can't treat me unfairly because I'm a foreigner [immigrant]. Just because I'm a foreigner [immigrant], I've always told myself that I have to work harder and do better, so that other people can't look down on me. I don't pick a fight at work. But, if you treat me unfairly, I'm gonna fight! You can't take advantage of me because I'm a foreigner [immigrant]!" Sue sought help from her union to mediate with her employer, and she eventually solved the salary equity issue.

In another case, Rachel, a fifty-year-old computer programmer at a public university, fought an unfair evaluation by her supervisor. When she received the poor work evaluation, she filed a grievance and argued her case to the dean. She recounted: "How can she [my supervisor] say that I 'showed no evidence of job competence' [in the evaluation]? I went to the dean and brought all the evidence of my work, including the records of all the presentations that I made at conferences and the computer system that I created for the university. I also went to the AAUP [American Association of University Professors] to seek help. I know I am a racial minority, but you cannot treat me unfairly! I have two master's degrees and I am very good at what I do. She was being unfair!"

With the AAUP's mediation, Rachel's case was solved eventually. Her dean overruled the negative evaluation submitted by her supervisor and granted Rachel a promotion. However, feeling unhappy about what happened, Rachel quit her job and found a similar position at another university. When I asked Rachel whether she attributed this unfair evaluation to her race, she immediately responded:

Of course it's because of my race! Although I have good education and excellent work performance, when I speak, people can hear my accent and know I'm not a native-speaker. It affects how people treat me. I'm an Asian immigrant woman. Very often, people do not take me seriously. They often push me over or ignore me. When I was making presentations, some commented that they did not understand me, and some were impatient to hear what I had to say because I was not speaking perfect English. So, I spent a lot of time working on my presentations and speaking skills. I use a lot of graphs in my presentations and always prepare some jokes to tell during my presentations. You've got to show that you have a sense of humor and that you know American culture to compensate for the shortcomings because of your immigrant status.

Rachel's narrative reveals the vulnerable position of Taiwanese immigrant women shaped by their race, gender, and immigrant status. The subjects' triple-layer disadvantage—non-White, nonmale, and non-native-English-speaking—poses various obstacles for career advancement. These disadvantages sometimes lead to prejudice and unfair treatment in the workplace, even in professional jobs. Most women take a confrontational approach to deal with unfair treatment, to demonstrate their abilities, and to reassure their authority. For instance, Mindy, a clerk for an importing company, confronted her boss directly about his biased work evaluation. Elena, a director for a nonprofit organization, asserted her authority when a White colleague challenged her. Tracy, a manager for an insurance company, asked for the promotion she thought she deserved.

Although most cases of perceived unfair treatment occurred between the subjects and their White bosses, one woman encountered resistance from a Chinese immigrant supervisee. Cindy was a forty-year-old scientist and manager at a large pharmaceutical company. She supervised ten employees, from diverse racial backgrounds, in the research sector. During our interview, Cindy stated that all her White male bosses were supportive, and her promotions were never delayed regardless of her status of being non-White, nonmale, and non-native-speaking. However, she once encountered dismissive attitudes from a Chinese immigrant coworker, as Cindy recalled:

> He just did not take me seriously. He did not complete the tasks that I assigned, and did not seem to care about the quality of his work. I know I'm a woman. In Chinese culture, women are considered inferior. I think that's why he didn't show much respect to me. But, I'm his boss. I have more work experience and higher education than him. He needs to listen to me and respect my authority. I tried to tell him in many different ways, but he just didn't get the message. Finally, I confronted him directly and asked him to do what I demanded, because "I am your boss," I said [smiles]. He changed his attitudes after that.

Cindy added that, initially, she was indirect in the way that she communicated with her supervisee, because her culture taught her to be polite, nice, and not to hurt others' feelings. After several unfruitful attempts, she decided to use the "American way" to solve the issue by directly pointing out the problem. In doing so, Cindy asserted herself and made sure that her supervisee followed her commands and respected her authority.

Like Cindy, some women experienced a learning curve when they adapted to the "American way"—acting aggressively, being vocal about what they wanted, and challenging unfair treatment. The women considered these characteristics contradictory to their Taiwanese cultural values, but essential for career success in the United States. Tracy, a fifty-two-year-old senior statistician and manager at an insurance company, explained that it took a very long time for her to learn how to speak up for herself and to ask what she wanted at work:

> Growing up [in Taiwan], we did not learn how to speak up and how to deal with confrontation. It's not our culture. Our parents

and teachers always taught us: Be polite, be nice, don't rock the boat, and that "Silence is gold." But it doesn't work here [in the United States]. In America, you've got to ask for what you want, or you would never get it. You've got to stand up for yourself and make a noise, or you would be passed over and pushed over. We didn't learn how to do these things in Taiwan, so it took me a very long time to learn and practice the American way. It's all about communication and how you present yourself to others. You have to tell your boss specifically that you want this particular position, and that you are good for it. I learned from observing how my White colleagues did it at work. It's the opposite of our culture, so I've come a long way to where I am today [being a manager]. Even now, I still need to prepare myself when I plan on talking to my boss about a promotion. It doesn't come naturally.

Learning the hard way to achieve her career goals, Tracy knew how difficult it could be for Asian women to succeed in white-collar professions. Therefore, she founded a nonprofit organization to help fellow immigrant women and their children develop leadership skills. In workshops she coordinated for the organization, Tracy emphasized the importance of adapting to American culture in white-collar occupations. Strongly believing in recognizing the contradictions of the two cultures, Tracy encouraged others to abandon their "cultural baggage," as she termed it, to succeed in American corporations. In her view, Americanness and Taiwaneseness are two sets of opposite traits. In fact, many professional subjects, both men and women, reported the disadvantages that Taiwanese culture brings to their work.

As I explained in chapter 2, Taiwanese cultural tradition highly values humility, reserved temperament, quietness, and relational harmony; it also condemns crafty language in self-expression and self-centeredness. For first-generation Taiwanese Americans who grew up in such a societal culture, switching to a different cognitive framing is not always easy. At times, it creates feelings of frustration and injustice when individuals realize that their cultural heritage is an obstacle to career advancement. In response to this realization, most male subjects I have interviewed reported accepting their marginalized position. Nevertheless, like Tracy, many women reported striving to assimilate into American culture and acting confrontationally when encountering unfair treatment in the workplace.[5]

Lisa was the only woman who used a soft approach in her confrontation to challenge unfair treatment at work. A retired computer programmer, she recalled a few instances when she went to her manager to contest unfair treatment:

> I feel, because I am an Asian woman, I am not taken seriously and my opinions are not valued as much as Whites'. One time, our manager [a White man] was collecting ideas for purchasing a new machine. I wrote a report to him, suggesting a particular model and explaining the details of that machine. But, he did not respond to my report. A few days later, a White colleague suggested the same model over lunch, our manager immediately took note of what he said and promised to buy the machine. I was furious. So, I went to my manager that afternoon and asked him why he responded differently when I and that White male colleague suggested the same model. He apologized to me, but insisted that it was because he thought my male colleague was more experienced than me. He had no idea that it was racial discrimination when he treated us differently.

Later, when Lisa was passed up for a promotion, she explained to her boss how her leadership style was different from that of her White colleagues. She recalled: "I explained to my boss that Asian women are very different when it comes to leadership. Whites often take credit for themselves and do a lot of self-promotion. On the contrary, Asian women share credit with their teammates and are modest about their own achievements. I told my boss: 'You must see my abilities and how I do things, rather than judging me in the same ways as how you see my White colleagues.' He finally saw how I got things done without showing off and being full of myself."

Lisa's patient explanation paid off. She received promotions twice in five years and was in a management position until she retired. When asked what motivated her to speak up for herself in these instances, Lisa attributed her actions to what she learned from her company's regular training on affirmative action and cultural diversity issues: "Thanks to the required training that my company held on a regular basis, I understood what racial discrimination was and felt okay to take action when it happened. I remember one time several colleagues were talking disrespectfully about racial minorities in the office. Although they did not target me, I was very angry. It was not right complaining about racial minorities in front of me. So, I talked to them about the wrongdoing and reported it to my boss." Lisa not only spoke up at her workplace, she also applied her knowledge of racial discrimination to the larger community and her children's schools, which is discussed later in this chapter.

Regardless of many successful negotiations in the workplace and subjects' confrontational tendencies, not every professional woman chose to challenge unfair treatment. Judy, a thirty-nine-year-old college professor, described an unpleasant interaction she had with a White male job candidate:

> It happened a few years ago, when my department was hiring a new assistant professor. As the practice for campus interviews at my school, each candidate had thirty-minute one-on-one meetings with faculty members. One afternoon, a candidate came to my office for his interview. He was tall, skinny, well-dressed, young, and White. As soon as he sat down, I briefly introduced myself and asked if he had any questions about our program that I could help answer. He responded vulgarly and impatiently in a sarcastic tone: "Why don't you cut the crap? Let's get to the point. What do you want to know about me?" He rolled his eyes and lifted up his chin as he spoke, dismissively

and disrespectfully. I was stunned by his ill-manner, egoism, and arrogance. Caught off-guard, I did not say anything critical back at that moment, but I kept thinking about why he treated me like that. Is it because I'm Asian and I'm a woman?

After carefully observing how the job candidate interacted with her colleagues, Judy realized that she was the only one who received "special treatment." Being the only woman of color in her department, she concluded that her gender, race, and immigrant status led to the candidate's dismissive attitudes and behaviors, although she was in an obviously more powerful position in the interview context.

Judy appeared angry when recalling this incident. She regretted that she did not say anything critical right away to teach that job candidate a lesson, but admitted that she was unprepared for the situation. She was afraid of bringing the issue up at her department meeting because several senior colleagues favored this candidate and she did not want to offend them by criticizing their top choice. At the time, Judy was untenured, so she felt compelled not to take any risks that could possibly damage her career, including speaking her mind. She explained how this incident changed her perspective about U.S. society and her place in it:

> It was a wake-up call for me. I used to believe in the American dream, believed in equality and egalitarianism—things that we don't have in Taiwan. I went to a graduate school [in the United States] where people cared about your intelligence but not your gender or race. I got my job because of my work regardless of the fact that I'm a foreigner [immigrant]. I used to believe that as long as I work hard and demonstrate my ability, I would earn people's respect and recognition. I thought I was just an individual, like everyone else in the United States. However, that encounter completely changed my perspective. I suddenly realized that I'm an Asian woman. Some people don't treat you with respect simply because of that. I have been sensitive about my race and gender ever since.

Another academic, Jamie, expressed her frustration about racist and sexist demeanors she encountered at her workplace:

> I have encountered some racial and gender prejudice. For example, a young male [White] colleague always turned his head away when I said "Hi" to him in the hallway. He's never looked at me in the eyes. It's like I don't exist in his eyes. He often dismissed my opinions at the department meeting by lifting up his chin, rolling his eyes, and looking at his watch. When I was talking, he always interrupted. He did not treat others the same way. Once, I mentioned this to a female [White] colleague, she said I thought too much because he did not treat her that way. I'm like, "Of course not! You are White!" The other day, a minority student came to my office and complained about a racist remark that colleague made in class. The student went to the department chair but was told he was "thinking too much" because that faculty claimed that he "was just joking." The student expressed his anger and feelings of vulnerability, sentiments that I am too familiar with. As an immigrant Asian woman, I sometimes sense prejudice in my encounters with people. But, these experiences are very difficult to validate and sometimes painful to describe. In most cases, I don't have "proof" that I am treated with prejudice, but you would know when you are treated without respect, and, it's not a pleasant feeling.

Like Judy, Jamie changed her viewpoint about American values of equality, which was why she came to the United States in the first place. Jamie did not think silence was the right solution, but she found it difficult to confront the prejudiced person because of her Asian cultural heritage and Christian beliefs. She also did not want to be perceived by her colleagues as a "crazy dragon lady," being difficult, or someone who "rocks the boat." Jamie explained her feelings of ambivalence:

> What can I do? Go to him and say "You're a jackass"? I wish I had the guts [laughing]! But then, he would deny [it], and

probably tell others that I'm a "crazy dragon lady"! Besides, my Asian culture raised me to be polite and tolerant, and my Christian teaching tells me to be forgiving. So, I often thought to myself that maybe he [the prejudiced White guy] just had a bad day. Well, he kind of has a bad day every time he sees me [smiles]! I think he doesn't know what he did is hurtful. I tried to find excuses for him. But, it's not easy to always strive to give the benefit of the doubt. I don't want my colleagues to think I'm difficult, as I have my reputation and career to think about. In my heart, I know I have been racially and sexually discriminated against. But in my head, I try to forgive him, even though I know he is a racist, sexist, arrogant jerk.

Both Judy's and Jamie's accounts exemplify the high emotional costs that Asian Americans and other people of color have to pay when experiencing racial prejudice and discrimination.[6] Unlike Whites, people of color often take an emotionally consuming journey to figure out what happens in a particular setting, and decide how to respond and validate recurring discriminatory incidents. Unlike Wendy and Rachel, who worked in practical fields that differed from their original professional training and who dared to take the risk of speaking up, Judy and Jamie were the few female professionals who stayed in the areas of their graduate studies. They had their careers in mind when pondering what to do in their encounters of racial prejudice and considered the stakes too high. Although Judy and Jamie were unable to confront prejudiced individuals directly, they became more sensitive to prejudice and discrimination. Both also reported that they became more sympathetic to other racial minorities, such as Hispanics and Blacks.

Everyday Racism

Subjects' gender, race, and immigrant status not only shape their vulnerable position in the workplace concerning their unfair treatment; these factors also lead to experiencing prejudice in their everyday lives. Linda, a fifty-three-year-old housewife, described her experience of everyday racism: "I helped out at my children's school a lot when they were young. Most teachers were very nice to me, although I spoke poor English. I think they appreciated my help. But, there were a few [White] parents who were very rude to me. We volunteered in the school library and worked together three days a week, but they never talked to me. There was a mother who was especially rude. When I said 'Hi' to her, she always turned her head away and pretended that she didn't see me. After a few times, I stopped saying 'Hi' to her." Another housewife, Sophia, reported a similar experience: "One of our neighbors is very unfriendly. We see each other very often because they live just behind us, and our children go to the same school. But, every time I said 'Hi', she just turned her head away. I don't know what her problem is. . . . Is it because I'm Asian? I don't know, but she is very unfriendly."

When asked what could cause such unfriendly attitudes, these housewives responded that race and immigrant status together shaped people's assumptions about them and, thus, affected their behaviors. Sophia explained, "Before they [Whites] get to know you, they have already assumed that you don't speak English and that you are uneducated, just because you are an immigrant home-maker. But, in fact, I have good education [bachelor's degree] and speak decent English. We live in this nice middle-class neighborhood, which indicates that we are a good family. But I guess some people just don't like foreigners [immigrants]. I feel that some Whites just don't want to have anything to do with you, even when you are neighbors."

Another highly educated homemaker, Gina, also received simi-lar treatment at a grocery store. Being a mother of two little children, Gina became a housewife after earning her master's degree in the United States. One day, while grocery shopping with her two children, her one-year-old daughter was cranky, crying and running around. Distracted, Gina misspoke something in her con-versation with the cashier. The cashier corrected her and advised her with a dismissive attitude: "You know, English is very difficult. You've got to work harder on your English so that you don't make a mistake like this."

Gina was mad. She wanted to complain to the store manager but, at that moment, her children were arguing and pushing each other. Suppressing her urge to fight over the unfair treatment, Gina decided to calm her children and take them home. She expressed regrets about not doing something about the prejudiced incident: "I feel very angry every time I think about this incident. Yes, I misspoke one word, but she [the cashier] treated me with this disrespectful, dismissive attitude. . . . it was like, she assumed that I was uneducated or illiterate. Even if I were uneducated or poor, I am a customer at the store. You cannot treat me like that! It's racism!" Harboring the anger resulting from this encounter, Gina swore that she would definitely go to the manager next time it happened. She also generalized that such prejudice often came from people of little education and of lower class.

While several subjects reported being discriminated against by cashiers at grocery stores, one woman was treated with prejudice while working as a cashier at a department store. Carol recalled her unpleasant experience with a Black customer when she worked in retail:

I worked at a high-end department store many years ago. One day, a Black guy came to the store to return something, but he didn't have the receipt. I said: "Let me see what I can do." When I entered the information, the computer system didn't allow me to do the return without the receipt. So, I explained the situation to him and said: "Let me get my manager to see what we can do for you." When my [White male] manager came, the guy complained to my manager: "I just want to return this, but this Chincky Wincky doesn't know what to do." My manager responded: "Sir, you cannot insult my employee that way." He got angry and started using foul language. He yelled at me: "You bitch!" I said to him, "I'm going to call security." When my manager picked up the phone and called security, he left.

Carol added that the racial slur did not offend her. She attributed this incident to what she termed the customer's "personal problem."

Nevertheless, a few years later when Carol was passed up for a promotion, she identified racism without hesitation. As Carol said:

> I thought I was the perfect candidate for the assistant manager position, based on my excellent job performance, work experience, and education. I am very fluent in English because I got my degree in England, so I couldn't think of anything that would have prevented me from getting that particular promotion. However, the company chose a White woman over me. I was so much better than her on everything, so the only reason I could think of was my race. I realized that there's no future for me in retail, no matter how hard I worked or how good I was. Racism was there. So, I quit.

Carol stayed home for a few years, until she began teaching Mandarin Chinese at a private school. She found an occupation in which her race was an advantage rather than an obstacle as she had experienced in White-dominant industries.

In everyday life, professional immigrant women also experience unfriendly attitudes and racial prejudice. Tiffany, a retired computer programmer, described an unpleasant encounter she had at a bookstore: "One day, as I was walking into a bookstore, I saw a [White] gentleman, who appeared to be in his early sixties, also coming toward the bookstore from the other end of the street. I held the door wide open to let him go inside before me. As he walked by, he looked at me and said: 'Do you know you must be able to read to come here?' I thought to myself, 'Aren't you supposed to say 'Thank you?' But, caught off-guard, I only responded with a wry smile. I wondered, would I be asked the same question if I were White?" Ann, a forty-one-year-old scientist at a pharmaceutical company, reported a similar experience of racial prejudice in her daily life:

> At work, people know that I am a scientist with a PhD, so I get the respect that I deserve. But, when I leave my workplace, it's a totally different story. Because I look Asian, people just assume

that I don't speak English and that I am uneducated. In fact, my education might be higher than most [White] people that I encounter in my daily life. One time, I was at a grocery store. As I was paying for my groceries, I asked the casher if they had Tic Tacs. The cashier didn't know what I meant, so I repeated "Tic Tacs" a few times. Finally, she got it and found a pack for me. Then, she mocked my accent and laughed with another cashier. I said to them: "Well, I know I speak English with an accent. That's probably because I speak four languages, so sometimes I don't pronounce every word precisely. How many languages do you speak, by the way?"

When Ann saw that the two cashiers looked embarrassed, she was glad that she did something for herself. She explained: "If they didn't look so embarrassed, I would go to their manager and complain about it. This is racism!"

Like Ann, most professional subjects used the term "racism" to conclude their accounts of experiences of prejudice. In contrast, housewives often identified their own immigrant status and language barriers as the cause of unfriendly attitudes from Whites. A few believed that insensitivity was revealed in these instances. For example, Kelly had earned a doctoral degree in education from a U.S. university. She taught part-time at a community college and spoke fluent English. However, she was often frustrated by what people assumed of her before getting to know her:

Because we look Asian, people have assumptions about you, especially when you are a woman. One day, my husband and I ran into a neighbor at the voting polls. The neighbor had talked to my husband before, but not me. She said to my husband: "Oh, I remember your wife. I remember seeing her in the neighborhood. She didn't speak English, so we didn't talk much." I thought to myself, "Well, we haven't had a chance to talk, how do you know that I don't speak English?" You cannot just assume that I don't speak English and that I am uneducated. This is very insensitive and ignorant!

Kelly also recalled an encounter with a staff member in the school district office when her family first moved to the predominantly White neighborhood: "When we first moved here, we went to the school district office to ask about the schools in the area. The [White] staff [member] who greeted us was very friendly. After an informative introduction, she said to us: 'This is a very nice area. We have very few racial minorities here, so it's very safe.' I was furious and responded: 'What do you mean? We are [a] racial minority.' She then apologized. I think she meant Blacks, not Asians, but that's not okay no matter which racial minority she referred to."

Frances, a fifty-year-old housewife, told a similar story concerning the lack of understanding about racial and cultural diversity among Whites:

One day, I was talking with some other parents about an academically gifted program in our school district while waiting for my son outside of his school. A teenager was there with her mom. We talked about some kids we knew who qualified for the program because they scored very high on the SAT. That girl said to her mom [in front of us]: "Do you know Tina Chen also qualified for the advanced ELA program? English is not even her language!" I was shocked by this comment, because Tina is second-generation Taiwanese who was born here [the United States]. English *is* her first language! But, Tina's White peer still considered her a foreigner!

Frances continued:

When my son was in sixth grade, he told me a girl at school asked him where he was from. He was confused by the question because he was born and raised here, just like that girl. Another kid lifted his eyes up with fingers and made fun of my son's "Chinese look." I had to explain to my son how people often mistake Asian Americans as foreigners, but it's incorrect. Besides, we are Taiwanese Americans, not Chinese or Chinese Americans. I also taught him that everyone looks different. It's *not* okay to tease people about their looks. I had a long talk with him about his cultural heritage and race in America.

Teaching the next generation about racial prejudice is a major challenge that immigrant mothers face. Mindy, a clerk at an importing company, described one situation:

One day, I was shopping with my eight-year-old son at a department store. When we walked by two female [White] store employees, we overheard them talking about Asians in a disrespectful way loudly. My son asked me: "Mommy, why do they talk about Asians that way? Did we do anything wrong to make them mad?" I went to the manager to report this incident. The manager apologized and promised to educate their employees about racial diversity issues. I had a long talk with my son that night about race. It was not an easy topic for an eight year old, and honestly, I'm not sure if he totally understood. I'm hoping that the incident did not leave a scar. He may encounter more difficult situations when he grows up. We must prepare him for that.

Another mother, Carol, talked about how she helped her son accept and appreciate his differences from his White peers:

I made mostly Asian food for my children's lunch when they were in elementary school. One day, my son came home crying. He told me a [White] girl made fun of his sushi lunch. In front of other kids, the girl said: "Yuck! That looks disgusting!" He was very sad. So, I told him: "Well, too bad, I don't think she has tried it before. Maybe you should tell her you have no idea what you're missing!" The next day, the same girl teased him again. He responded: "Oh, you don't know what you are missing. This is the best thing ever! Oh, my goodness, it's so yummy! Yum. . . . yum!" That girl has never said anything afterwards.

Carol turned this incident into a teachable moment to help her children understand why people say negative things about others and how to handle similar situations in the future.

Mothers reported various situations in which they taught their children to be proud of their cultural heritage and to accept who they are. Among these mothers, Lisa was particularly active. She was a computer programmer at a large information technology company that conducted extensive employee training on affirmative action policies and racial diversity issues. One day, her second-grade daughter came home crying because some kids at school called her names and made fun of her Asian looks. Lisa went to the principal the next day to discuss this matter:

> I asked the principal if the school had resources to train
> teachers about affirmative action and cultural diversity
> issues. He said no. He said that it's [the] parents' responsibility,
> not the school's, to teach their children how to interact with
> racial minorities. I disagreed. I told him about how my
> company provided employees with resources and training to
> increase their awareness and sensitivity around racial minorities.
> I believed that schools can and should do the same. So, I dis-
> cussed this matter with my boss and asked what we could do.
> My company began to provide consultation and resources to
> local schools and helped train teachers about diversity issues.
> We also organized a parents' network to provide input and
> support.

Lisa's initiation and active involvement promoted public education on racial diversity issues in local schools and the community. Many White parents joined the network and worked alongside minority families to advocate for respect and appreciation of cultural diversity.[7] The network later extended their efforts to promote diversity among teachers and to help recruit teachers of color for public schools. Although Lisa began learning about diversity issues as a middle-aged woman, she successfully applied what she learned from her workplace to the larger community.

Growing up in a single-race society, these Taiwanese immigrants did not need to deal with race-related issues until they moved to the United States. Although not always easy, many of the women quickly learned the value of equality and acted upon what they considered the "American spirit." In varied contexts, women encountered racial prejudice in both the workplace and society. Their experiences offered reflections on their place in U.S. society and influenced how they educated the next generation. Rather than dwelling on their marginal position as Asian immigrants, most subjects took action to battle unfair treatment and reclaim their equal rights as Americans. These experiences also deepened their understanding of racial inequality and helped them develop empathy for other racial minorities.

Negotiating Race, Gender, and Citizenship

Previous studies have argued that Asian American women are more deprived compared to their male counterparts because of their double disadvantage as nonmale and non-White.[8] Such double disadvantage leads to Asian women's marginalized status in the labor force, as it entraps them in vulnerable positions. Patriarchal and racist ideologies consign Asian women to a secondary and inferior position in the capitalist wage-labor market. As a result, they experience the work world as both gendered and racialized individuals, and they obtain fewer economic resources compared to their male counterparts across social classes.[9]

Taiwanese immigrant women are positioned in a more disadvantaged position than native-born Asian women because of their foreign-born status in addition to being non-White and nonmale. Thus, race, gender, and immigrant status shape a triple disadvantage for Taiwanese immigrant women. Not only patriarchal and racist ideologies but also ethnocentric attitudes create multiple layers of inequality. Regardless of women's middle-class backgrounds and professional skills, they encounter prejudice and unfair treatment in the workplace and the larger society, including at their children's schools, in their neighbourhoods, and at stores.

For non-White immigrants, skin color, language barriers, and foreign accents are easy markers of racial others. In various contexts, these women are assumed to lack fluency in English or are mocked for their foreign accent. As Rosalind Chou and Joe Feagin argue, language mocking reveals social discrimination against racialized others, because it is usually Asian and Spanish but not European accents that are ridiculed in U.S. society.[10] Linguistics scholar Rosina Lippi-Green also points out that foreign accents only evoke negative reactions when they are linked to non-White or third-world populations. Therefore, discrimination based on accent perpetuates unequal power relations in a society.[11]

Facing multiple structural inequalities and disadvantages shaped by their race, gender, and foreign-born status, the Taiwanese immigrant women in this study exhibit behaviors that contradict stereotypes of Asian women as submissive, quiet, and willing to endure hardships. Most subjects take action to contest inequality and challenge unfair treatment. Even some housewives who lack fluency in English maintain their American pride and protest everyday racism. These actions evidently violate Confucian cultural norms that cultivate qualities of deference and quietness; they also provide a clear contrast with subjects' obedient and tolerant behaviors in their in-law interactions.

How do the women account for their progressive behaviors? When explaining their active approach to combating prejudiced treatment, subjects often highlighted their American identity and their values associated with this identity. Examples of common responses include "This is America, you cannot treat me unfairly"; "I am American, just like you [the prejudiced person]. So, you've got to respect me"; "In America, you need to be vocal about what you want and speak up for yourself"; "In the U.S., everyone is equal"; and "When people ask where I'm from, I always say Chicago. I am American. They can't just assume that I'm a foreigner."

These statements reveal the women's cultural assimilation and the salience of their American identity in the work domain and the public sphere. Subjects behave according to what they consider American values, and they speak up for their entitled individual rights as American citizens. Although recognizing their perceived status by Whites as Asian immigrant women, subjects choose to act "like Americans." By contesting unfair treatment, the women demonstrate their citizen status to those who treat them as "the other." This act of an *American self* brings a sense of empowerment; it also exemplifies subjects' racial performativity.

In social psychology, status construction theory argues that shared cultural beliefs of status (e.g., gender, race, social class, age, occupation) frame individuals' perceptions, behaviors, and social interactions. When people from different categorical groups interact with each other, hierarchies of respect and influence develop. Consequently, social differences often become status distinctions in relational contexts, which, in turn, reproduce and potentially modify structural inequalities.[12]

Status construction theory is useful in understanding Taiwanese immigrant women's proactive actions in their encounters with inequality. These women's American selves frame their cognition in perceiving their status in relation to Whites. Whites (and other Americans) may treat Asian immigrant women based on their Asian, female, and foreign-born status and the prejudice associated with that status. Nevertheless, these women refuse to accept this *White racial frame*, in Joe Feagin's term.[13] Rather, subjects see themselves as American citizens and act in ways that they consider an individual American would act in a discriminatory situation. In other words, in their racial performativity the women endeavor to challenge their designated "othered" status by demonstrating their identified Americanness.

Moreover, previous studies have observed that immigrant women from patriarchal societies gain a greater sense of independence, emancipation, and equality in Western societies, where individual autonomy and women's rights are valued more so than they are in their societies of origin.[14] Similarly, Taiwanese immigrant women learn Western egalitarian ideologies in the host society, especially in large corporations where diversity and inclusion issues are taken seriously and legally regulated. Such cultural exposure facilitates the women's senses of self-worth and independence in

American society. This newly gained autonomy is exhibited in the women's confrontational approaches to race-related issues in the work domain and the public sphere.

In *The Myth of the Model Minority*, Chou and Feagin discuss how Asian Americans' lack of collective memories of racial oppression leads to ambivalent and uncertain feelings of discrimination. Many in their study hesitate to identify racism in evidently discriminative encounters.[15] In *Our Separate Ways*, Ella Bell and Stella Nkomo report that Black women managers are more prepared than their White female counterparts when encountering discrimination because they grew up in a culture of racial oppression and resistance. Black women are also more vocal about injustices than White women, but they more readily acknowledge their marginalized position as outsiders because racial inequality is not new to their life world.[16]

Taiwanese immigrant women in my study provide a contrast to these two studies. Although lacking race-related experiences growing up in Taiwan, my subjects recognize racism without hesitation, and the majority take action to challenge unfair treatment. Although not all women are vocal about injustice, they resist their marginalized position as racial others. Growing up in a patriarchal society, the women develop new senses of justice and equality after migrating to the United States. As they assimilate into middle-class America, these women also gain a new identity as Americans. This newly evolved sense of self—what I call an *American self*—shapes their perceptions and behaviors in their many unpleasant encounters with prejudice and discrimination.

Conclusion

More than a century ago, W.E.B. Du Bois wrote about the double consciousness that African Americans constantly experienced being both American and Black.[17] Subjects in my study experience multiple consciousness in their lives in the United States—being Asian, female, immigrant, not native speakers of English, and American (even though the American part is often denied or overlooked by Whites and other Americans). However, this does not mean that these social identities are equally prominent in their lived experiences at all times. Rather, place, the nature of social relations, and the involved social actors' demographic characteristics shape which part(s) of consciousness becomes salient in individuals' cognitive frameworks and, thus, affect their behaviors in particular social contexts.

In the workplace and the larger society, racial and linguistic differences significantly mark subjects' experiences of their American lives. In these two social spheres, Taiwanese immigrant women's skin color and accents make their race and foreign-born status quickly identifiable. Gender becomes less salient in such contexts, and citizenship is far less evident. As I explain in chapter 1 on Mead's theory, individuals develop minds through role taking; they make behavioral choices and give meaning to their choices based on how they understand their roles, social contexts, and interactions with others. At work and in the public domain, American culture serves as a dominant ideology that provides the women with a cultural toolkit to comprehend their position in relation to others in American contexts. In particular, many professionals who work in corporations learn specific definitions of racism and receive training aimed at promoting equality. The women's narratives depict various racialized experiences, through which subjects illustrate their perceptions of who they are in relation to Whites, how they make sense of interracial interactions and their own behaviors. Their accounts of racial prejudice and discrimination reflect their acculturated perspectives, which assimilate to the public discourse in mainstream American society.

In contrast, gender is much more relevant than race in the women's consciousness in their one-race/ethnicity immigrant families (sometimes both gender and age are relevant; see chapter 5). Family is an important social institution where individuals find their sense of belongingness, security, and satisfaction. In particular, family serves as the foundation for immigrants' resistance against racial inequality in the larger society. It is also the major social domain within which immigrants preserve their traditional cultures, religions, and languages. Therefore, cultural changes within the family are less likely to take place than in the public sphere.

Furthermore, the women's work trajectories may influence how they perceive potential risks to challenging unfair treatment. As Wendy clearly pointed out, she had worked in many occupations that she had no background in and retreating to family was always an option. Therefore, she did not think of the possibility of being fired for speaking up as a threat that prevented her from seeking justice. Similarly, many professional women who work in high-demand fields due to changes immigration creates in their work-family contexts appear more willing to take chances. In addition, as revealed in Lisa's story, professional women's workplace training about affirmative action and racial diversity provides them with the vocabulary to speak up against racial discrimination, not only at work but also in other public contexts, such as their children's schools and grocery stores. Formal policies on diversity in American corporations and channels for filing grievance may also give these women a sense of security if they choose to report mistreatment at work.

In contrast, as I report elsewhere, Taiwanese immigrant men refuse to risk their career advancement to challenge racial inequality at work.[18] As their families' primary breadwinners, they have much to consider when weighing the potential costs if they contest the status quo. The thought that they could possibility lose their jobs or create hurdles for future promotion opportunities stops men from speaking up against racial discrimination. They remain silent and accept their marginalized position. As a Taiwanese immigrant man in my previous study said: "It's normal to be discriminated against. We are Asian anyway. It's part of American reality."

In summary, subjects' intersectional position, which is shaped by race, gender, foreign-born status, and citizenship, influences their self-perceptions in relation to Whites (and other Americans) in the workplace and in the larger society. Their postimmigration employment experiences also influence how they perceive racial inequality and the risks they may run to speak up against injustice. In this chapter, I document various social contexts in which women experience racial inequality and their reactions to the perceived unfair treatment. In most cases, these women use their American identities and values to define unjust situations; these identities and values also guide their behaviors.

Like other people of color, Taiwanese immigrant women encounter prejudice and discrimination at work and in their daily lives. They are not exempt from racial and gender inequalities in spite of their middle-class status; however, most subjects take action to contest structural inequality and speak up for their individual rights. The women's negotiations for equal treatment demonstrate their sense of an *American self*, which generates feelings of empowerment in their multiple-disadvantaged social position. Over time, the women acquire better understanding of racism and sexism, develop more empathy for other racial minorities because of their own personal experiences, and continue to fight for their dignity and respect in racialized America.

7
Suffering and the Resilient Self

After migrating to the United States, I have been through a lot of changes and difficulties, and I struggled enormously. It's not an easy life here, but I have grown a lot. I have become a better person—more independent, more patient, more empathetic, and more grateful. I have become a person that I like better than before [immigration]. After all these years, I have come to a realization that whenever there are difficulties, there are turning points. Suffering has deeply shaped my endurance and resilience.
—Stacie, 62, MBA, computer programmer, divorcée

In a community study in Los Angeles, California, 12 percent of Korean American women across social class were diagnosed with anger disorder, three times higher than that of their counterparts in South Korea (4.2 percent).[1] Yun-Jung Choi discusses this finding and highlights immigration experience as a major factor that contributes to Korean women's anger. She reports that Korean immigrant women experience a great deal of social, psychological, physical, and spiritual stress in their adaptation processes in the host society as they adjust to a new culture, new language, and new societal environment. Meanwhile, Korean Confucianism continues to place patriarchal norms on the family, demanding women's submission and suppressed emotions. Confucian gender role expectations constitute another significant cause of Korean immigrant women's anger, especially after they are exposed to egalitarian gender culture in the United States.[2] These studies suggest that the drastic changes immigration brings to life could generate fairly negative effects on women's well-being, even for those in the middle class.

Although no similar study has been conducted about Taiwanese American women's mental health condition, the challenges in adaptation and the cultural clashes in immigrant lives are not difficult to imagine. In this book, I document many struggles and adjustments that highly skilled Taiwanese American women experience throughout their life courses and within different social domains. International migration creates new work-family contexts that not only restructure the women's lives but also reconstruct their senses of self through the numerous ups and downs in their adaptation processes. Their narratives of these journeys provide rich information to discuss the multifaceted connections of immigration, gender, work, family, culture, social class, race and ethnicity, citizenship, and the self.

Gendered Immigration, Work-Family, Self, and Well-Being

Most subjects in this study migrate as dependents when their U.S.-trained husbands secure professional jobs in the United States. Many give up high-status, high-paying jobs in Taiwan to unite their families in the host society. Restricted by their dependent visas, these women cannot work during the initial phase of their family settlement. Therefore, they are tied closer to the domestic sphere in a gendered process I call *housewifelization*. The division between work and family is consequently intensified. In contrast to their husbands who continue their pursuits of higher education and career, these women are positioned in a new work-family context that interrupts their career trajectories. In other words, gendered immigration creates a clear breadwinner and homemaker division in middle-class Taiwanese families. These new housewives tend to consider housework and childcare their sole responsibilities because of their unemployment status.

Many women find themselves lost in their new lives as unemployed immigrant housewives—this sense of *lost self* is a result of their housewifelization. They struggle with feelings of boredom, isolation, emptiness, and loss of purpose. Some become clinically depressed, and a few become suicidal. Mourning their lost careers and missing the loved ones they left behind, these women search intensively to build new senses of self and redefine the meanings of employment and housework as they adapt to the host society.

In spite of their husbands' strong opposition, some women work illegally just to go out and explore the world. *Misemployment* often occurs—a former high school teacher takes a data-entry job, works night shifts, and earns minimum wage; a former corporate secretary waits tables; a former middle school teacher works as a babysitter; a former city government staff member cleans hotel rooms; and a former prosecutor washes dishes for a university cafeteria. These women's families do not need their incomes for survival or upward mobility, but the women find gratification and happiness in working outside of their homes.

After the women become permanent residents, two pathways emerge in their choices of work. Some remain homemakers for the rest of their lives and find satisfaction in their children's achievements and developing close family bonds. A great number of women enter the U.S. labor force, usually in practical fields such as accounting and computer programming. As a result, the meaning of work changes. Employment becomes jobs that bring income, instead of careers that fulfill their passions as in their professions before immigration. Both groups of women express a sense of nostalgia in their *imagined self* when fantasizing what they would have become had they not migrated to the United States. None of the housewives imagine themselves being housewives, but successful career women in Taiwan. In contrast, professional women dream about working in the fields of their original training in Taiwan. However, these women are also aware of the more severe and pervasive gender discrimination in their home country that could hinder their career pursuits.

In the early years of subjects' family settlement, gender and immigration interact to create new work-family contexts that affect the women's perceptions of who they are, their gender roles, employment options, and the careers they left behind. As they build their new lives as immigrants, they also reconstruct new meanings of work, family, and self.

Culture, Family Structure, and Gender Performance

The family is an important institutional foundation for immigrants' survival, prosperity, and resistance against racial inequality in the larger society. It is also a major social sphere where most immigrants find senses of security, satisfaction, and belongingness. In this book, I examine two familial relations in middle-class Taiwanese immigrant families: spousal relations and in-law relations.

The gender division of domestic labor and decision-making power on family budgets are two key indicators for measuring gendered power relations in the family. While subjects shoulder most of the housework, the majority jointly or solely manage family finances. The women use both cultural interpretations and practical reasoning to explain who does what around the house. Less than one-third of subjects believe that housework is a woman's job. However, this traditional gender ideology is more prevalent among men and mothers-in-law who consider men doing housework shameful and a violation of Confucian gender norms.

Most women use practical reasoning to rationalize their division of labor at home. Their explanations show practical considerations based on either employment status or skills. In many homemakers' perceptions, employment status creates a territorial boundary between work and family. Because they are home all day, they are in charge of all domestic matters, including cleaning, cooking, child raising, and family finances. This perspective—what I call the *domestic self*—leads to their willingness to voluntarily take care of all household chores. At the same time, they have greater control over decisions on family budgets and financial investments. In contrast, employed women do not succeed in using the same reasoning to negotiate more sharing from their husbands. Married men often use Confucian culture to defend their exemption from domestic work, a traditional gender ideology that is further reinforced by their mothers.

Individual skills and abilities are another type of practical reasoning uncovered in subjects' rationalizations. Many women explain that they are better than their husbands at financial management, so they oversee family budgets and stock investments. This perspective justifies women's controlling power over family finances even though they are not the primary breadwinners. It also shows a sense of empowerment and pride, what I call the *capable self.* Women's accounts of their roles in the family suggest that gender ideology or culture is not the only validation for their gender practices at home. Women's economic resources also do not always affect their status in the family, as other studies of immigrant families have suggested.

In the few families that share housework equally, couples began their fair division of labor very early in the relationship and engaged in little or no negotiation over time. These women are aware of their husbands' cultural deviance and often describe their spouses as atypical or nonconventional. These couples continue to face social pressure in their ethnic community because of their nonconformity to traditional gender practice.

Many Taiwanese immigrants live with the husband's parents who demand traditional gender roles and filial obedience from the couple, especially the wife. In these three-generation households, the unreasonable requests and verbal abuse by mothers-in-law often lead to tensions, deteriorating spousal relationships, and women's damaged self-esteem. In-laws impose the most patriarchal oppression on married Taiwanese immigrant women, even those in the most egalitarian marriages. Both men and women feel compelled to abide by Confucian teachings of filial piety and act dutifully in the presence of the husband's parents and siblings. In particular, mothers-in-law often demand submission and quietness from their daughters-in-law. Although feeling stressed and furious, most women choose to tolerate in-law inequality and domination for the sake of their families' well-being.

Women's employment status provides different resources to cope with in-law stress and the consequent marital tension at home. Professionals are able to stay in their offices for long hours and take out-of-town business trips to reduce their time at home. Some seek counseling to release their anger and feelings of injustice. In contrast, some housewives reported driving around town for hours to calm down and discharge their frustrations. They also complain to fellow immigrant women and seek social support from their ethnic community. These different strategies achieve varied levels of success.

While some husbands are supportive of their wives, they also highly value filial piety and feel compelled to conform to traditional cultural norms. Thus, both men and women retain their overt submission to the husband's parents. When the women turn to their own mothers for advice, they are told to endure any pain that comes with their role as daughters-in-law. When the women turn to coethnics for support, they receive understanding and empathy; however, they are also advised to remain obedient to their in-laws. Confucian gender norms are repetitively reinforced, as a firm cultural belief in the status hierarchy between mothers-in-law and daughters-in-law persists in the Taiwanese immigrant community.

Moreover, Taiwanese in-law inequality is further sustained by several intertwined structural and social-psychological factors: (1) Moving overseas excuses immigrant couples from their filial duties, which creates feelings of guilt. Hosting in-law guests, to some extent, compensates for such guilty feelings. (2) Subjects' middle-class statuses allow them to host guests without financial concerns. (3) In one-race/ethnicity families, no contesting ethnic cultures exist to offer alternative social norms. (4) Family as a private sphere leaves little room for competing gender ideologies. (5) The women gain symbolic capital and earn their husbands' gratitude by acting as filial daughters-in-law. As a result, married women continue to perform Confucian patriarchy by enduring inequality and concealing their true emotions. In other words, the daughter-in-law's *silenced self* in her emotion work is mandatory to achieve relational harmony in three-generation households.

Although privileged by their social class, Taiwanese American women are a visible racial minority in the United States because of their skin color, a status they acquire only after immigration. Their accents also make their foreign-born status quickly identifiable. Subjects in this study encounter prejudice and mistreatment both in the workplace and in the larger society. At work they are given trivial tasks and their opinions are devalued. Some receive biased work evaluations, are paid less than their White colleagues in the same positions, and are treated disrespectfully by some coworkers. In their everyday lives, these women are often mocked for their foreign accents, are assumed to be uneducated, and are ignored by neighbors and other parents at their children's schools. Their native-born children are also assumed to be foreign and considered "others" by peers and their parents.

In response, most subjects, including those housewives who speak little English, act confrontationally to contest prejudice and mistreatment. Their progressive behaviors contradict Confucian values of womanhood—being submissive and quiet—and challenge stereotypes of Asian women. The women highlight their American identity when explaining how they perceive their encounters with racial prejudice and their reactions to mistreatment. They assert that every American is entitled to protect one's own rights and speak up against injustice. Acknowledging the multiple disadvantages of their race, gender, and foreign-born status, subjects consciously choose to act how they consider American citizens would act when handling unfair treatment. Therefore, their experiences of racialization in the United States tell many stories about taking action to protest against racialization, through which their *American self* is manifested in their racial performativity.

Intersectional Social Structure and Lived Experiences

Taiwanese American women's life stories, as documented in this book, provide rich data to discuss the varied ways that interlocking structural factors shape individuals' lived experiences. International migration as a gendered process creates new work-family contexts in the lives of highly skilled Taiwanese women when they arrive in the United States as dependents. As the women begin their adaptation in the host society, different structural factors intersect to shape various aspects of their lives. The intersection of gender, immigration, work, and family is most evident during the early years of the women's settlement. The women's dependent visa status and the financial risks they take (i.e., giving up their own sources of income and pursuits of career) when they migrate are also very real structural factors that profoundly change their lives. The reconfiguration of the postimmigration social structure shapes the choices available to the women, and it reconstructs their senses of self through the process of making choices about work, family, and their own future.

While traditional cultural expectations of gender roles continue to influence spousal relations, the work-family boundary and individual abilities play important roles that govern and justify gender practices. Confucian culture constitutes the most confining social force in three-generation households and demands married women's submission. However, such cultural dominance is sustained by several interlocking structural and social-psychological factors, including immigration, social class, race and ethnicity, gender, age, place, symbolic capital, emotional economies, and emotion work. Women's employment and their ethnic community provide resources to create coping strategies to mitigate distress. Race, gender, and foreign-born status intersect to situate subjects in a disadvantaged position that makes them vulnerable to prejudice and discrimination both in the workplace and in the larger society. Nevertheless, American citizenship grants the women a sense of legitimacy and entitlement to fight against injustice.

In other words, the elements of the social structure that become significant in shaping individuals' experiences and their intersectional effects are complex social phenomena. No single factor can explain such complexities. Grounded in the women's standpoints, this book unveils some of the complex social phenomena by illuminating the women's understandings of themselves in relation to others and their surroundings, the life chances presented to them under structural constraints, their dilemmas and struggles, and their choices of action in varied situated contexts.

From Suffering to Resilience

When I started this project almost ten years ago, my focus was to document Taiwanese American women's suffering in their immigration journeys. Several dozen interviews later, what I found in their life stories was resilience. Uprooting themselves from the world with which they were familiar to start a new life in a foreign land, the women encountered numerous challenges and, at times, struggled tremendously. As they realigned themselves in the new society, they also found hope and new opportunities for their family prosperity, unexpected work trajectories, and self-growth.

French sociologist Pierre Bourdieu and American anthropologist Arthur Kleinman use the term *social suffering* to describe human responses to social problems caused by political factors, economic conditions, institutional power, and social disparities.[3] The stories presented in this book similarly highlight the interconnection of social environment and human struggles where the battlefield of power and inequality manifests itself. More important, the women's social suffering reveals much more than just structural power and inequality and its effects on individuals' well-being. Throughout the women's narratives of social suffering, their resilience and endurance is often brought to center stage.

As detailed in this book, misemployment and housewifelization caused by immigration does not stop the women's determination to find niches for themselves in the host society. Many overcome cumulative disadvantage and reenter the labor force, while some prioritize their family obligations and find satisfaction in their children's achievements. The women's burden of housework does not overshadow their sense of capability in managing family finances. Their surrendering to the in-law hierarchy does not prevent them from seeking emotional outlets. The women's multiple disadvantages due to their non-White, non-male, and non-native-born status do not silence their voices as American citizens. These women's stories beautifully exemplify how individuals exert agency under structural constraints and in the midst of life struggles.

As conveyed in Stacie's heartfelt reflexive account of her journey from Taiwan to the United States quoted in the beginning of this chapter, international migration has brought numerous challenges and struggles to the women's lives; but it also has helped nurture their inner strength and self-growth. Therefore, we see Wendy's bravery in standing up to her bully supervisor, Jen's patience in preserving her family regardless of her in-laws' domination, Ann's boldness in questioning the cashier who mocks her foreign accent, and Dolly's courage in leaving her abusive husband in spite of her coethnics' imposing advice to stay. As Stacie said, "Whenever there are difficulties, there are turning points." It is often in the women's deepest sorrows and despairs that we see the beauty and strength of human endurance. In the women's emotional engagement with themselves as they face the difficulties and pain in life, resilience is built and cultivated.

Appendix
Demographic Information of Subjects

PSEUDONYM	AGE	EDUCATION	OCCUPATION
Alice	30	MA	marketing consultant at telecommunications firm
Amy	30	MA	intern psychologist/housewife
Ann	41	PhD	scientist at pharmaceutical company
Aurora	57	high school	self-employed salon owner and stylist
Beth	44	MA	researcher
Blair	48	BA	housewife
Carol	47	BA	professional Chinese teacher
Cindy	40	PhD	scientist at pharmaceutical company
Christine	40	MBA	housewife
Dolly	50	BA	realtor
Elena	56	BA	project director at public service institute
Eliz	50	BA	accountant at airline company
Erin	53	MBA	accountant
Frances	50	MS	housewife
Gina	50	MBA	housewife
Jamie	43	PhD	college professor
Jen	50	BA	business owner
Joy	60	professional diploma	housewife
Judy	39	PhD	college professor
Katie	61	BS	computer programmer
Kelly	44	EDD	adjunct college professor/housewife
Kristi	51	BA	computer programmer
Lauren	39	BA	computer programmer

(continued)

PSEUDONYM	AGE	EDUCATION	OCCUPATION
Linda	53	professional diploma	housewife
Lisa	61	PhD	retired computer programmer
Marcia	52	MA	retired computer programmer
Marge	56	BA	statistician
Mary	62	MA	retired computer programmer
Michelle	41	professional diploma	housewife
Mindy	39	MS	clerk at importing company
Molly	50	BA	bank teller
Nicole	60	BA	retired computer programmer
Patty	62	professional diploma	realtor
Rachel	50	MA	computer programmer
Rebecca	54	MA	travel agent
Rose	53	BA	part-time math tutor/housewife
Ruth	49	BA	housewife
Selena	49	MA	architect
Sophia	60	BA	housewife
Stacie	62	MBA	computer programmer
Sue	56	BA	pharmacy technician
Tara	55	MA	label designer
Tiffany	52	MA	retired computer programmer
Tracy	52	MA	statistician/manager at insurance company
Wendy	54	BS	computer programmer

Acknowledgments

A decade ago, I began studying Taiwanese Americans with the objective of discovering the major sources of their stress and coping mechanisms. After finishing my first book on gender differences among Taiwanese Americans, I was fascinated by the women's stories. Their immigration journeys are full of unexpected turns. Their lives reveal much about how social structure constrains individuals' options but, at the same time, enables various means of resisting, negotiating, and challenging the imposition of power. I still vividly remember those sleepless nights in Chicago when I pondered over my subjects' life histories. I felt heartache about these women's adversities, but also found inspiration in their courage and strength in facing their life struggles. I am indebted to all the women who spent many hours telling me their immigration experiences, adaptation difficulties, and reflexive perspectives about their lives in the United States. It is my sincere hope that this book documents the complexity of their lived experiences.

This project received financial support from the Chiang Ching-Kuo Foundation and Western Michigan University, for which I am thankful. Many colleagues at WMU have cordially supported my work. I am especially grateful to my department chair, David Hartmann, for a course release that allowed me to complete this book. I thank the two anonymous reviewers for their insightful comments that helped me sharpen my argument. Lisa Banning at Rutgers University Press was very helpful and patient throughout the process. Colleen Moore proofread several drafts of this book. Taiwanese American artist Yu-Ru Huang gave me permission to use her art as the book cover, and Patrick Huang helped her describe the spirit of the art. I appreciate their support.

Many friends have been important in both my intellectual and personal lives, for whom I am forever grateful. Rita Gallin trained me with the highest standards and enthusiasm in graduate school. She is the role model I look up to when guiding students' research. Steve Gold has graciously given me valuable advice and opportunities to further my career. Brendan Mullan taught me how to teach and has been an inspiration in academia. I am thankful for their support and friendship. Several friends have been great sources of support and inspiration: Brooke Kelly, Nancy Mesey, Heather Dillaway, Manashi Ray, and Pauline Acosta. I am appreciative of their continuous encouragement and friendship over the years.

Finally, I would not have been able to finish this book without the unfailing support from my wonderful husband, Yuan-Kang Wang. As a scholar himself, Y. K. understands the time and energy required for research, and he has shouldered much of the housework and child-raising responsibilities so I could focus on writing. He has given me the space and partnership I need to pursue my passion. Our two sons, Kevin and John, are precious sources of joy in our family life. They always make me laugh and keep reminding me of the need to have fun when I am stressed out. Seeing their smiling faces brings light, peace, and happiness to my life.

Notes

1 Introduction

1. Curran et al. 2006; Espiritu 2002; Gu 2012; Hondagneu-Sotelo 2003, 2013; Pedraza 1991; Pessar 2003.
2. Gu 2012.
3. These female- and labor-intensive industries have rapidly grown since the late 1960s, which has brought a significant number of immigrant women laborers to the United States (Clement and Myles 1994; Hossfeld 1994).
4. Baker 2004; Grasmuck and Pessar 1991; Kibria 1993; Lim 1997; Pessar 1984.
5. Ehrenreich and Hochschild 2002.
6. Hondagneu-Sotelo 1994.
7. Chen 1992; Espiritu 2002; George 2005; Gu 2006; Min 1998; Pesquera 1993.
8. Phizacklea 1983.
9. Min 2001.
10. Kim and Hurh 1988; Min 1992.
11. Kang 2010.
12. Pearce, Clifford, and Tandon 2011.
13. Gu 2012.
14. Grzywacz et al. 2005.
15. Gerson 2004.
16. Grasmuck and Pessar 1991; Kibria 1993; Lim 1997; Min 2001; Pessar 1984.
17. Morokvasik 1984.
18. Gu 2014.

19. Purkayastha (2005) uses the term *cumulative disadvantage* to describe varied barriers highly skilled women encounter in their attempts to enter the U.S. labor force and build their careers when they migrate as dependents.

20. Brettell and Simon 1986.

21. Hartsock 1983.

22. Smith 1987.

23. Harding 1991.

24. Collins (1990) 2000.

25. McCall 2005; Weber 2010.

26. Hekman 1997.

27. Haraway 1988.

28. Thomas and Znaniecki (1918) 1984.

29. Handlin (1951) 1973.

30. Stonequist (1937) 1961.

31. Gold 1997.

32. Mead (1934) 1967.

33. Stryker 1980.

34. Giddens 1991.

35. Goffman 1959.

36. My previous project (Gu 2006) examines major sources of stress in the lives of Taiwanese Americans. I interviewed fifty-four subjects in the greater Chicago area, including twenty-seven men and twenty-seven women. Twenty of the subjects were second-generation and thirty-four were first-generation Taiwanese immigrants.

37. Atkinson 1998.

38. Glaser and Strauss 1967.

2. Immigration, Culture, Gender, and the Self

1. Chen 1992.

2. Tseng 1995.

3. Ng 1998.

4. Gu 2006.

5. Most notably, Chen reports that approximately 20 to 25 percent of Taiwanese immigrants in the United States are Christian, greatly exceeding

the small portion of Christians in Taiwan (3.9 percent). In addition, most Buddhists said they converted only after immigration, although Buddhism is traditionally a dominant religion in Taiwan (Chen 2010).

6. For instance, in one episode, the mother emphasizes the importance of academic excellence. When her oldest son receives an A, she goes to the principal and complains that the schoolwork is too easy. When asking her children to study after school, the mother points at a few White kids playing outside and tells her children that those kids will not succeed because they are wasting their lives playing. However, what is on her children's mind is the longing to go outside and join their friends. This story may reinforce the tiger mom image and the public stereotype that Asian children are forced to study and are not allowed to have fun.

7. Immigrants from China to Taiwan are from two ethnic groups. Pre-1949 Chinese immigrants are primarily from Fujian and Guangdong Provinces and speak Taiwanese and Hakka, respectively. They comprise the majority of the population on the island and became the so-called *benshegnren*. Having lived in Taiwan for centuries, *benshengren* consider themselves "local people" of Taiwan and tend to embrace a strong Taiwanese identity. Post-1949 Chinese immigrants are called Mainlanders or *waishengren*. They speak Mandarin and tend to embrace a Chinese identity. *Waishengren* immigrants in the United States socialize more with Chinese immigrants, whereas *benshengren* immigrants tend to maintain a Taiwanese identity. The Taiwanese immigrant women I interviewed are from both groups.

8. U.S. Bureau of the Census 2010a.

9. U.S. Bureau of the Census 2000, 2003, 2007, 2010a.

10. Holdaway 2007.

11. Chen 1992; Ng 1998.

12. Ng 1998; Ward 2006.

13. Gu 2013.

14. Chang 1992.

15. Gu 2012.

16. Portes and Rumbaut 1996.

17. U.S. Bureau of the Census 2003.

18. U.S. Bureau of the Census 2010b.

19. Holdaway 2007.

20. Ward 2006.

21. Chee 2005.

22. Asian American Center for Advancing Justice 2012.

23. Confucianism was taught in the class on "Life and Ethics" in elementary schools and in "Citizenships and Morality" in middle schools before 2001. In both classes, students learned major cultural values and behavioral norms in Confucianism (Apple Daily News, July 31, 2006; accessed May 6, 2016, www.appledaily.com/tw/appledaily/article/deadline/20060731/2786397.)

24. After the removal of these subjects, many parents and teachers complained about students' lack of ethics and bad behavior. In 2004, the public began to advocate for the Ministry of Education to bring Confucian teaching back to formal education (Apple Daily News 2006). In response, Taiwan's Ministry of Education created a new subject, Central Ethics, in the elementary and middle schools. This class teaches students important Confucian values such as honesty, diligence, collectivism, dignity, and self-discipline (Ministry of Education, Taiwan. www.edu.tw).

25. Yao 2000.

26. Gallin 1995; Yu 2001.

27. Yao 2000.

28. Republic of China Ministry of Justice, 2013, Criminal Code of the Republic of China (amended date: 2013. 6.11), *Laws & Regulations Database of the Republic of China* (Taipei, Taiwan: Ministry of Justice). Accessed September 12, 2013, http://law.moj.gov.tw/Eng/LawClass/LawAll.aspx?PCode=C0000001 and http://law.moj.gov.tw/LawClass/LawAll.aspx?PCode=C0000001.

29. Hu 1995.

30. Ibid.

31. Gu and Gallin 2004.

32. Lan 2006.

33. Gallin 1986; Stacey 1983; Wolf 1972.

34. Stacey 1983, 54.

35. Lau 1992.

36. Ibid., 3.

37. "Silence is gold" is an old saying in Taiwanese society. The Taiwanese cultural tradition highly values humility; it also condemns crafty

language in self-expression. Silence is considered a presentation of humility; it also implies tolerance, a characteristic that is highly valued in Taiwanese culture. The cultural aphorism, "Empty vessels make the most sound," means when a person knows little, he or she needs to brag with crafty words to cover up his or her ignorance. In contrast, a person who is full of knowledge is usually quiet and self-reserved.

38. Yao 2000.
39. Swidler 1986.
40. Gu 2006, 2010.
41. Faist 2000a.
42. Manohar 2013.
43. Park 2009.
44. Espiritu 2002.
45. These observations are from my field notes. For instance, while at the ladies' lunch gathering, a Taiwanese mother tried to explain to others why she allowed her daughter to participate in the school musical. During the conversation, Chinese mothers tried to convince her that "it's useless," "it's a waste of time," "it's not classical music," and "it would not help her college application." I later talked with this Taiwanese mother in private. She expressed her self-doubts in parenting because of the enormous pressure she felt from other (Chinese) mothers. At these mothers' gatherings, women often discussed what sports and musical instruments their children played, and how to prepare their children for college applications. Chinese and Taiwanese mothers showed different attitudes and perceptions of children's activities.
46. Patterson 2014.
47. Bondi 2002.
48. Conradson and McKay 2007.
49. Faist 2000b.
50. Giddens 1979.
51. Foucault 1980, 142.
52. Lorber 1994; Risman 1998.
53. Wolf 1992.
54. Gu 2006.

3. Searching for Self in the New Land

1. Teaching jobs are one of the most esteemed occupations in Taiwan. This social attitude is rooted in Confucianism, which ranks intellectuals, farmers, industry workers, and businessmen as four major occupations in society. Intellectuals are ranked first in this hierarchical order, and intellectuals who teach are considered agents of knowledge and morally superior to others. A popular aphorism, *yiri weishi zhongsheng weifu*, exemplifies the cultural belief that students should respect teachers as children respect their parents (*When someone is your teacher for a day, he or she should be respected like your parent forever*).

2. In earlier days (1960s to early 1980s), it was widely believed in Taiwan that America was "paved with gold." Working in the United States was considered a golden opportunity.

3. Taiwan's educational system is extremely competitive. Students must pass rigid entrance exams in order to attend the best high schools, colleges, and graduate schools. Starting in elementary school, students are given an enormous amount of homework almost daily, even during summer and winter breaks. Extracurricular activities, including sports and music, are not encouraged. In such an environment, academic performance is often considered the major criterion of one's worth. Although there have been some educational reforms in the past decade to reduce students' academic stress, the value of academic achievements continues to dominate Taiwanese culture.

4. In contrast, lower-class Taiwanese immigrants are determined to permanently stay in the United States (Gu 2006, 2014).

5. Massey 1986.

6. Castles and Miller 1998; Massey 1986.

7. Since immigration is seldom a one-time event but rather a social process, it is important to differentiate individual motives for initial immigration and permanent settlement (Gu 2006, 2014).

8. Amit and Riss 2007; Gold 1997; Gu 2014.

9. Gu 2006, 2014.

10. See Alberts and Hazen 2005; Amit and Riss 2007; Gold 1997; Gu 2006, 2014; Gubhaju and Jong 2009; Jensen and Pedersen 2007; Liu-Farrer 2009; Murakami 2009. Only three of these studies (Gu 2006, 2014;

Gubhaju and Jong 2009) analyze how gender affects immigration motives.

11. Gu 2014.

12. Gu 2006.

13. In Taiwanese culture, a husband's residence is considered part of the patrilineal side's property. Therefore, the husband's parents and siblings often believe that they can visit and stay as long as they wish. In contrast, the wife's relatives usually stay only for a few days when visiting the couple because they perceive themselves as guests or outsiders.

14. Although this is a very common pattern, there are exceptions. For instance, a female subject applied for babysitting jobs in the United States in the 1970s, because she was determined to leave Taiwan due to its political instability. She worked several laborer jobs before becoming a hairdresser. She remained single and lived alone in suburban Chicago. Another subject came to pursue a PhD in chemistry. She wanted to work in the United States, so her husband followed her and found a job nearby. Another female subject began to work after earning her master's degree while waiting for her husband to finish his studies. She planned to return, but her husband insisted that their family settle in the United States. These cases suggest the complexities of immigration motives and processes. Throughout the book, I report exceptions wherever suitable to show that although major patterns can be found in the study, individuals' lived experiences are by no means homogeneous.

15. Purkayastha 2005.

16. Diggs 1998; Kurotani 2005; Yasuike 2011.

17. Korean soap operas are very popular in Taiwan. Many shows with Chinese captions are available on the Internet.

18. Yasuike 2011.

19. See Grasmuck and Pessar 1991; Kibria 1993; Lim 1997.

20. However, these husbands make important educational decisions for their children, such as college applications.

21. Gold 1997, 410.

22. See similar arguments in previous studies conducted in the United States (Purkayastha 2005; Yasuike 2011), Denmark (Liversage 2009), Australia (Ho 2008), Canada (Man 2004), and New Zealand (Meares 2010).

4. Negotiating Egalitarianism

1. As I have argued elsewhere (Gu 2006, 2012, 2015a), multiple indicators are needed to capture the complexity of spousal power relations and the multiple aspects of family life. In my previous study (Gu 2006), I used four variables, the gender division of domestic labor, decision-making power on family settlement, decision-making power on family finances, and decision-making power on children's education, to explore various facets of spousal power relations.
2. Blood and Wolf 1960.
3. Baker 2004; Espiritu 2002; Grasmuck and Pessar 1991; Kibria 1993; Lim 1997; Pessar 1984.
4. Baker 2004; Foner 1986; Smith and Mannon 2010.
5. Four of these women's ex-husbands did not pay child support at all. Two supported their children financially only occasionally, giving one hundred dollars from time to time. One woman had to work two jobs after her divorce to support her children's education.
6. Grasmuck and Pessar 1991; Kibria 1993; Min 2001; Pessar 1984.
7. Grasmuck and Pessar 1991; Kibria 1993; Min 2001; Pessar 1984.
8. Hochschild 1989.

5. Performing Confucian Patriarchy

1. Confucian principles of filial piety demand children's absolute obedience and complete devotion to parents. These principles also apply to daughters-in-law, as they are part of the patrilineal household (also see chapter 2).
2. The concept of *emotional economy* refers to how individuals' behaviors and feelings are influenced by the cultural ideologies concerning what family members owe to or are owed by other members (Shih and Pike 2010).
3. In contrast, most women did not use this cultural explanation to describe their spousal relationships (see chapter 4).
4. Shih and Pike 2010.
5. Applying Goffman's dramaturgical perspective, I coin the term *situational patriarchy* to describe the staged performances of patriarchy that

Taiwanese immigrant men and women engage in when they are in different contexts (Gu 2009).

6. Hochschild 1983.
7. Gu 2006.
8. Gu 2006.
9. Ridgeway 2011.

6. Fighting for Dignity and Respect

1. See chapter 3 for the work-family contexts of highly skilled immigrant women and their work trajectories.
2. See Gu (2006, 2010). Previous studies also report similar findings. Immigrant women from patriarchal societies gain a greater sense of independence, emancipation, and equality in Western societies, in which individual autonomy and women's rights are valued more so than in their societies of origin (Ho 2008; Kibria 1993; Lim 1997; Pessar 1984).
3. Gu 2015b.
4. Male subjects react to racial inequality differently from their female counterparts (Gu 2006). Although men and women professionals identify their race as a major barrier to their career advancement, men accept their othered position in relation to their White colleagues and perceive racial inequality as a normal part of U.S. society. Some believe that it is too late for them to change their Taiwaneseness, and hope the next generation will become more American and more assimilated into mainstream culture.
5. This effort is limited to the work domain. In the family, most women intend to preserve Taiwanese cultural values, especially in their generational relations.
6. Feagin and Sikes 1994.
7. According to Lisa, the school district had approximately 9 percent Asian and 1 percent Black students.
8. Espiritu 1997; Man 2004; Shin and Chang 1988.
9. Chai 1987; Espiritu 1997; Hossfeld 1994; Raijiman and Semyonov 1997; Shin and Chang 1988; Yamanaka and McClelland 1994.
10. Chou and Feagin 2010.
11. Lippi-Green 1997.

12. Ridgeway 1991, 2006; Ridgeway and Correll 2004; Ridgeway and Kricheli-Katz 2013.

13. Feagin (2013) uses the term *White racial frame* to discuss how Americans of color are pressured to conform to a White-imposed framework, a racial hierarchy in which Whites are generally the privileged group.

14. Ho 2008; Kibria 1993; Lim 1997; Pessar 1984.

15. Chou and Feagin 2010.

16. Bell and Nkomo 2001.

17. Du Bois (1903) 1989.

18. Gu 2015b.

7. Suffering and the Resilient Self

1. Lin et al. 1992.

2. Choi 2015.

3. Giddens 1999; Kleinman, Das, and Lock 1997.

References

Alberts, Heike C., and Helen D. Hazen. 2005. "'There Are Always Two Voices . . .': International Students' Intentions to Stay in the United States or Return to Their Home Countries." *International Migration* 43 (3): 131–152.

Amit, Karin, and Ilan Riss. 2007. "The Role of Social Networks in the Immigration Decision-Making Process: The Case of North American Immigration to Israel." *Immigrants & Minorities* 25 (3): 290–313.

Asian American Center for Advancing Justice. 2012. "A Community of Contrasts: Asian Americans, Native Hawaiians, and Pacific Islanders in the Midwest." Washington, DC: Asian Americans Center for Advancing Justice.

Atkinson, Robert. 1998. *The Life Story Interview.* New York: Sage.

Baker, Phyllis L. 2004. "'It Is the Only Way I Can Survive': Gender Paradox among Recent Mexicana Immigrants to Iowa." *Sociological Perspectives* 47: 393–408.

Bell, Ella Louise J., and Stella M. Nkomo. 2001. *Our Separate Ways: Black and White Women and the Struggle for Professional Identity.* Boston: Harvard Business School Press.

Blood, Robert O., and Donald M. Wolf. 1960. *Husbands and Wives.* Glencoe, IL: Free Press.

Bondi, Liz. 2002. *Subjectivities, Knowledges, and Feminist Geographies: The Subjects and Ethics of Social Research.* Lanham, MD: Rowman and Littlefield.

Brettell, Caroline B., and Rita Simon. 1986. "Immigrant Women: An Introduction." In *International Migration: The Female Experience*, edited by Rita J. Simon and Caroline B. Brettell, 3–20. Totowa, NJ: Rowman and Allanheld.

Castles, Stephen, and Mark J. Miller. 1998. *The Age of Migration: International Population Movements in the Modern World*. London: Macmillan.

Chai, Alice Y. 1987. "Freed from the Elders but Locked into Labor: Korean Immigrant Women in Hawaii." *Women's Studies* 13: 223–234.

Chang, Shirley L. 1992. "Causes of Brain Drain and Solutions: The Taiwan Experience." *Studies in Comparative International Development* 27: 27–43.

Chee, Maria W. L. 2005. *Taiwanese American Transnational Families: Women and Kin Work*. New York: Routledge.

Chen, Carolyn. 2010. *Getting Saved in America*. Princeton: Princeton University Press.

Chen, Hsiang-Shui. 1992. *Chinatown No More: Taiwan Immigrants in Contemporary New York*. Ithaca: Cornell University Press.

Choi, Yun-Jung. 2015. "The Impact of Gender, Culture, and Society on Korean Women's Mental Health." *Social Behavior and Personality* 43 (4): 593–600.

Chou, Rosalind S., and Joe R. Feagin. 2010. *The Myth of the Model Minority: Asian Americans Facing Racism*. Boulder, CO: Paradigm Publishers.

Clement, Wallace, and John Myles. 1994. *Relations of Ruling: Class and Gender in Postindustrial Societies*. Montreal: McGill-Queen's University Press.

Collins, Patricia Hill. (1990) 2000. *Black Feminist Thought*. London: Routledge.

Conradson, David, and Deirdre McKay. 2007. "Translocal Subjectivities: Mobility, Connection, Emotion." *Mobilities* 2 (2): 167–174.

Curran, Sara R., Steven Shafer, Katharine M. Donato, and Filiz Garip. 2006. "Mapping Gender and Migration in Sociological Scholarship: Is It Segregation or Integration?" *International Migration Review* 40: 199–223.

Diggs, Nancy. 1998. *Steal Butterflies: Japanese Women and the American Experience*. Albany: State University of New York Press.

Du Bois, William E. B. (1903) 1989. *The Souls of Black Folk*. New York: Bantam.

Ehrenreich, Barbara, and Arlie R. Hochschild. 2002. "Introduction." In *Global Woman*, edited by Barbara Ehrenreich and Arlie R. Hochschild, 1–14. New York: Metropolitan Books.

Espiritu, Yen Le. 1997. *Asian American Women and Men*. London: Sage.

———. 2002. "Filipino Navy Stewards and Filipina Health Care Professionals: Immigration, Work, and Family Relations." *Asian and Pacific Migration Journal* 11: 47–66.

Faist, Thomas. 2000a. "Transnationalization in International Migration: Implications for the Study of Citizenship and Culture." *Ethnic and Racial Studies* 23 (2): 189–222.

———. 2000b. *The Volume and Dynamics of International Migration and Transnational Social Spaces.* Oxford: Clarendon Press.

Feagin. Joe R. 2013. *The White Racial Frame: Centuries of Racial Framing and Counter-Framing.* 2nd ed. London: Routledge.

Feagin, Joe R., and Melvin P. Sikes. 1994. *Living with Racism: The Black Middle-Class Experience.* Boston: Beacon Press.

Foner, Nancy. 1986. "Sex Roles and Sensibilities: Jamaican Women in New York and London," In *International Migration: The Female Experience*, edited by Rita J. Simon and Caroline B. Brettell, 133–151. Totowa, NJ: Rowman and Allanheld.

Foucault, Michel. 1980. *Power/Knowledge: Selected Interviews and Other Writings 1972–1977.* London: Vintage/Penguin Books.

Gallin, Rita S. 1986. "Mothers-in-Law and Daughters-in-Law: Intergenerational Relations within the Chinese Family in Taiwan." *Journal of Cross-cultural Gerontology* 1: 31–49.

———. 1995. "Engendered Production in Rural Taiwan: Ideological Bonding of the Public and Private." In *Engendering Wealth and Well-Being: Empowerment for Global Change*, edited by Rae L. Blumberg, Cathy A. Rakowski, Irene Tinker, and Michael Monteon, 113–134. Boulder, CO: Westview Press.

George, Sheba. 2005. *When Women Come First.* Berkeley: University of California Press.

Gerson, Kathleen. 2004. "Understanding Work and Family through a Gender Lens." *Community, Work and Family* 7: 163–178.

Giddens, Anthony. 1979. *Central Problems in Social Theory: Action, Structure and Contradiction in Social Analysis.* London: Macmillan.

———. 1991. *Modernity and Self-Identity.* Stanford: Stanford University Press.

———. 1999. *The Weight of the World: Social Suffering in Contemporary Society.* Cambridge: Polity Press.

Glaser, Barney G., and Anselm L. Strauss. 1967. *The Discovery of Grounded Theory*. New York: Aldine De Gruyter.

Goffman, Erving. 1959. *The Presentation of Self in Everyday Life*. New York: Anchor Books.

Gold, Steve. 1997. "Transnationalism and Vocabularies of Motive in International Migration: The Case of Israelis in the United States." *Sociological Perspectives* 40: 409–427.

Grasmuck, Sherri, and Patricia R. Pessar. 1991. *Between Two Islands: Dominican International Migration*. Berkeley: University of California Press.

Grzywacz, Joseph G., Sara A. Quandt, Thomas A. Arcury, and Antonio Marin. 2005. "The Work-Family Challenge and Mental Health: Experiences of Mexican Immigrants." *Community, Work and Family* 8: 271–279.

Gu, Chien-Juh. 2006. *Mental Health among Taiwanese Americans: Gender, Immigration, and Transnational Struggles*. New York: LFB Scholarly Publishing.

———. 2009. "Situational Patriarchy: Gender Relations among Taiwanese Immigrants." Paper Presented at the Annual Meeting of the American Sociological Association, San Francisco.

———. 2010. "Culture, Emotional Transnationalism, and Mental Distress: Family Relations and Well-Being among Taiwanese Immigrant Women." *Gender, Place and Culture* 17 (6): 687–704.

———. 2012. "Women's Status in the Context of International Migration." *Sociology Compass* 6 (6): 458–471.

———. 2013. "Taiwanese Americans." In *Multicultural America*, edited by Carlos E. Cortés and J. Geoffrey Golson, 2043–2044. Thousand Oaks, CA: Sage.

———. 2014. "Contextualizing Vocabularies of Motive in International Migration: The Case of Taiwanese in the United States." *International Migration* 52 (2): 158–177.

———. 2015a. "The Gendering of Immigration Studies in the United States." *Advances in Gender Research* 20: 269–289.

———. 2015b. "Racial Glass Ceilings, Gendered Responses: Taiwanese American Professionals' Experiences of Otherness." *Sociological Focus* 48: 126–149.

Gu, Chien-Juh, and Rita S. Gallin. 2004. "Taiwan." In *The Encyclopedia of Sex and Gender: Men and Women in the World's Cultures*, edited by

Carol R. Ember and Melvin Ember, 848–857. New York: Kluwer Academic Publishers.

Gubhaju, Bina, and Gordon F. De Jong. 2009. "Individual versus Household Migration Decision Rules: Gender and Marital Status Differences in Intentions to Migrate in South Africa." *International Migration* 47 (1): 31–61.

Handlin, Oscar. (1951) 1973. *The Uprooted*. Boston: Little, Brown.

Haraway, Donna J. 1988. "Situated Knowledges: The Science Question in Feminism and the Privilege of Partial Perspective." *Feminist Studies* 14: 575–599.

Harding, Sandra. 1991. *Whose Science? Whose Knowledge?* Ithaca: Cornell University Press.

Hartsock, Nancy C. M. 1983. "The Feminist Standpoint: Developing the Ground for a Specific Feminist Historical Materialism." In *Discovering Reality: Feminist Perspectives on Epistemology, Metaphysics, Methodology, and the Philosophy of Science*, edited by Sandra Harding and Merrill Hintikka, 283–310. Dordrecht, Netherlands: Reidel.

Hekman, Susan. 1997. "Truth and Method: Feminist Standpoint Theory Revisited." *Signs: Journal of Women in Culture and Society* 22: 341–365.

Ho, Christina. 2008. *Migration and Gender Identity: Chinese Women's Experiences of Work, Family, and Identity in Australia*. Saarbrücken: VDM Verlag.

Hochschild, Arlie Russell. 1983. *The Managed Heart: Commercialization of Human Feeling*. Berkeley: California University Press.

———, with Anne Machung. 1989. *The Second Shift: Working Parents and the Revolution at Home*. New York: Viking Press.

Holdaway, Jennifer. 2007. "China: Outside the People's Republic of China." In *The New Americans: A Guide to Immigration since 1965*, edited by Mary C. Waters and Reed Ueda, 355–370. Cambridge: Harvard University Press.

Hondagneu-Sotelo, Pierrette. 1994. *Gendered Transitions: Mexican Experiences of Immigration*. Berkeley: University of California Press.

———. 2003. "Gender and Immigration: A Retrospective and Introduction." In *Gender and U.S. Immigration: Contemporary Trends*, edited by Pierrette Hondagneu-Sotelo, 3–19. Berkeley: University of California Press.

———. 2013. "New Directions in Gender and Immigration Research." In *The Routledge International Handbook of Migration Studies*, edited by Steven Gold and Stephanie Nawyn, 180–188. New York: Routledge.

Hossfeld, Karen J. 1994. "Hiring Immigrant Women: Silicon Valley's 'Simple Formula'." In *Women of Color in U.S. Society*, edited by Maxine Baca Zinn and Bonnie T. Dill, 65–93. Philadelphia: Temple University Press.

Hu, Yow-hwey. 1995. *Three Generation Cohabitation? Myth and Trap* [in Chinese]. Taipei: Chu Liu.

Jensen, Peter, and Peder J. Pedersen. 2007. "To Stay or Not to Stay? Out-Migration of Immigrants from Denmark." *International Migration* 45 (5): 87–112.

Kang, Miliann. 2010. *The Managed Hand: Race, Gender, and the Body in Beauty Service Work*. Berkeley: University of California Press.

Kibria, Nazli. 1993. *Family Tightrope*. Princeton: Princeton University Press.

Kim, Kwang Chung, and Won Moo Hurh. 1988. "The Burden of Double Roles: Korean Wives in the U.S.A." *Ethnic and Racial Studies* 11: 151–167.

Kleinman, Arthur, Beena Das, and Margaret Lock, eds. 1997. *Social Suffering*. Berkeley: University of California Press.

Kurotani, Sawa. 2005. *Home Away from Home: Japanese Corporate Wives in the United States*. Durham, NC: Duke University Press.

Lan, Pei-Chia. 2006. *Global Cinderellas: Migrant Domestics and Newly Rich Employers in Taiwan*. Durham, NC: Duke University Press.

Lau, D. C., trans. 1992. *Confucius: The Analects*. Hong Kong: Chinese University Press.

Lim, In-Sook. 1997. "Korean Immigrant Women's Challenge to Gender Inequality at Home: The Interplay of Economic Resources, Gender, and Family." *Gender and Society* 11: 31–51.

Lin, Keh-Ming, John K. C. Lau, Joe Yamamoto, Yan-Ping Zheng, Hun-Soo Kim, Kyu-Hyoung Cho, and Gayle Nakasaki. 1992. "Hwa-Byung: A Community Study of Korean Americans." *Journal of Nervous & Mental Disease* 180: 386–391.

Liu-Farrer, Garcia. 2009. "Educationally Channeled International Labor Mobility: Contemporary Student Migration from China to Japan." *International Migration Review* 43 (1): 178–204.

Lippi-Green, Rosina. 1997. *English with an Accent*. New York Routledge.

Liversage, Anika. 2009. "Vital Conjunctures, Shifting Horizons: High-Skilled Female Immigrants Looking for Work." *Work, Employment and Society* 23 (1): 120–141.

Lorber, Judith. 1994. *Paradoxes of Gender*. New Haven, CT: Yale University Press.

Man, Guida. 2004. "Gender, Work and Migration: Deskilling Chinese Immigrant Women in Canada." *Women's Studies International Forum* 27: 135–148.

Manohar, Manita N. 2013. "Mothering for Class and Ethnicity: The Case of Indian Professional Immigrants in the United States." *Advances in Gender Research* 17: 159–185.

Massey, Doug S. 1986. "The Settlement Process among Mexican Migrants to the United States." *American Sociological Review* 51: 670–685.

McCall, Leslie. 2005. "The Complexity of Intersectionality." *Signs: Journal of Women in Culture and Society* 30 (30): 1771–1800.

Mead, George H. (1934) 1967. *Mind, Self, and Society*. Chicago: University of Chicago Press.

Meares, Carina. 2010. "A Fine Balance: Women, Work and Skilled Migration." *Women's Studies International Forum* 33: 473–481.

Min, Pyong Gap. 1992. "Korean Immigrant Wives' Overwork." *Korean Journal of Population and Development* 21: 23–36.

———. 1998. *Changes and Conflicts: Korean Immigrant Families in New York*. Needham Heights, MA: Allyn and Bacon.

———. 2001. "Changes in Korean Immigrants' Gender Role and Social Status, and Their Marital Conflicts." *Sociological Forum* 16: 301–320.

Morokvasik, Mirjana. 1984. "Birds of Passage Are Also Women." *International Migration Review* 18 (4): 886–907.

Murakami, Yukiko. 2009. "Incentives for International Migration of Scientists and Engineers to Japan." *International Migration* 47 (4): 67–91.

Ng, Franklin. 1998. *The Taiwanese Americans*. Westport, CT: Greenwood Press.

Park, Keumjae. 2009. *Korean Immigrant Women and the Renegotiation of Identity*. El Paso, TX: LFB Scholarly Publishing.

Patterson, Orlando. 2014. "Making Sense of Culture." *Annual Review of Sociology* 40: 1–30.

Pearce, Susan, Elizabeth J. Clifford, and Reena Tandon. 2011. *Immigration and Women: Understanding the American Experience*. New York: New York University Press.

Pedraza, Silvia. 1991. "Women and Migration: The Social Consequences of Gender." *Annual Review of Sociology* 17: 303–325.

Pesquera, Beatriz M. 1993. "'In the Beginning He Wouldn't Lift a Spoon': The Division of Household Labor." In *Building with Our Hands: New*

Directions in Chicano Studies, edited by Adela De la Torre and Beatriz M. Pesquera, 181–195. Berkeley: University of California Press.

Pessar, Patricia R. 1984. "The Linkage between the Household and Workplace of Dominican Women in the U.S." *International Migration Review* 18: 1188–1211.

———. 2003. "Engendering Migration Studies: The Case of New Immigrants in the United States." In *Gender and U.S. Immigration: Contemporary Trends*, edited by Pierrete Hondagneu-Sotelo, 20–42. Berkeley: University of California Press.

Phizacklea, Annie, ed. 1983. *One Way Ticket: Migration and Female Labour*. London: Routledge.

Portes, Alejandro, and Rubén G. Rumbaut. 1996. *Immigrant America: A Portrait*. Berkeley: University of California Press.

Purkayastha, Bandana. 2005. "Skilled Migration and Cumulative Disadvantage: The Case of Highly Qualified Asian Indian Immigrant Women in the U.S." *Geoforum* 36: 181–196.

Raijiman, Rebeca, and Moshe Semyonov. 1997. "Gender, Ethnicity, and Immigration: Double Disadvantage and Triple Disadvantage among Recent Immigrant Women in the Israeli Labor Market." *Gender & Society* 11 (1): 108–125.

Ridgeway, Cecilia L. 1991. "The Social Construction of Status Value: Gender and Other Nominal Characteristics." *Social Forces* 70 (2): 367–386.

———. 2006. "Status Construction Theory." In *Contemporary Social Psychological Theories*, edited by Peter J. Burke, 301–323. Stanford: Stanford University Press.

———. 2011. *Framed by Gender: How Gender Inequality Persists in the Modern World*. Oxford: Oxford University Press.

Ridgeway, Cecilia L., and Shelley J. Correll. 2004. "Unpacking the Gender System: A Theoretical Perspective on Cultural Beliefs and Social Relations." *Gender & Society* 18: 1162–1167.

Ridgeway, Cecilia L., and Tamar Kricheli-Katz. 2013. "Intersecting Cultural Beliefs in Social Relations: Gender, Race, and Class Binds and Freedoms." *Gender & Society* 27 (3): 294–318.

Risman, Barbara. 1998. *Gender Vertigo: American Families in Transition*. New Haven, CT: Yale University Press.

Shin, Eui H., and Kyung-Sup Chang. 1988. "Peripheralization of Immigrant Professionals: Korean Physicians in the United States." *International Migration Review* 22: 609–626.

Shih, Kristy Y., and Karen Pike. 2010. "Power, Resistance, and Emotional Economies in Women's Relationships with Mothers-in-Law in Chinese Immigrant Families." *Journal of Family Issues* 31 (3): 333–357.

Simon, Rita J., and Caroline Brettell, eds. 1986. *International Migration: The Female Experience.* Totowa, NJ: Rowman and Allanheld.

Smith, Dorothy. 1987. *The Everyday World as Problematic: A Feminist Sociology.* Boston: Northeastern University Press.

Smith, Rebecca A., and Susan E. Mannon. 2010. "'Nibbling on the Margins of Patriarchy': Latina Immigrants in Northern Utah." *Ethnic and Racial Studies* 33 (6): 986–1005.

Stacey, Judith. 1983. *Patriarchy and the Socialist Revolution in China.* Berkeley: University of California Press.

Stonequist, Everett V. (1937) 1961. *The Marginal Man: A Study in Personality and Culture Conflict.* New York: Russell and Russell.

Stryker, Sheldon. 1980. *Symbolic Interactionism: A Social Structural Version.* Menlo Park, CA: Benjamin Cummings.

Swidler, Ann. 1986. "Culture in Action: Symbols and Strategies." *American Sociological Review* 51: 273–286.

Thomas, William I., and Florian Znaniecki. (1918) 1984. *The Polish Peasant in Europe and America.* Urbana: University of Illinois Press.

Tseng, Yen-Fen. 1995. "Beyond 'Little Taipei': The Development of Taiwanese Immigrant Businesses in Los Angeles." *International Migration Review* 29: 33–58.

U.S. Bureau of the Census. 2000. "Foreign-Born Profiles (STP-159)." Washington, DC: U.S. Department of Commerce.

———. 2003. "The Foreign-Born Population: 2000." Washington, DC: U.S. Department of Commerce.

———. 2007. "American Community Survey." Washington, DC: U.S. Government Printing Office. Accessed November 10, 2008, http://www.census.gov/acs/www/index.htm

———. 2010a. "The Foreign-Born Population." Washington, DC: U.S. Department of Commerce.

————. 2010b. "American Community Survey Briefs." Table 3. Washington, DC: U.S. Department of Commerce.

Ward, Annita Marie. 2006. "Taiwanese Immigrants." In *Immigration in U.S. History*, edited by Carl L. Bankston III and Danielle A. Hidalgo, 655–657. Pasadena, CA: Salem Press.

Weber, Lynn. 2010. *Understanding Race, Class, Gender, and Sexuality.* 2nd ed. Oxford: Oxford University Press.

Wolf, Diane Lauren. 1992. *Factory Daughters: Gender, Household Dynamics, and Rural Industrialization in Java.* Berkeley: University of California Press.

Wolf, Margery. 1972. *Women and the Family in Rural Taiwan.* Stanford: Stanford University Press.

Yamanaka, Keiko, and Kent McClelland. 1994. "Earning the Model-Minority Image: Diverse Strategies of Economic Adaptation by Asian-American Women." *Ethnic and Racial Studies* 17: 79–114.

Yao, Zinzhong. 2000. *An Introduction to Confucianism.* Cambridge: Cambridge University Press.

Yasuike, Akiko. 2011. "Economic Opportunities and the Division of Labor among Japanese Immigrant Couples in Southern California." *Sociological Inquiry* 81 (3): 353–376.

Yu, Wei-Hsin. 2001. "Family Demands, Gender Attitudes, and Married Women's Labor Force Participation: Comparing Japan and Taiwan." In *Women's Working Lives in East Asia*, edited by Mary C. Brinton, 70–95. Stanford: Stanford University Press.

Index

Foucault, Michel, 36
Framed by Gender (Ridgeway), 125–126
Frances (housewife), 61, 107, 114, 117,
144–145

Gary (Wendy's supervisor), 128, 163
gender: culture and—, 36, 94, 157–159;
family norms and—(*see* gender,
norms); framework for defining self/
others, 125; immigration, 41–45, 58
(*see also* immigration/immigrant);
inequality, 5, 8, 81 127, 147–150, 156, 160;
norms, 1–2, 23–26, 65, 69–72, 78, 84,
87, 92–94, 99, 110, 114, 120, 123–125, 154,
157–158; social construction of, 37, 126.
See also gender roles
gender roles: culture-based interpretations, 73, 74–80; effects of immigration,
13, 14, 155–157; family finances, 88–94
(*see also* finances); gendered division of
work and family, 3, 6, 45–66, 67, 73–87,
92, 157–158; negotiating egalitarianism, 69–94; patriarchal nature, 29;
practical reasoning, 73, 80–86; reversal
of, 3, 86–88; traditional, 49, 60–61, 97,
101–111, 116. *See also* Confucian cultural
values; gender
Giddens, Anthony, 10, 36
Gina (housewife), 56, 61, 65, 107, 112–113,
140–141
glass ceiling, 54
Goffman, Erving, 10, 11, 111, 178n5
Gold, Steve, 9, 67
gratitude, emotion of, 109
green card. *See* visa status
Greg (Mary's husband), 46–47
grounded theory, 14
guilt, feelings of, 76, 123–124, 159

Handlin, Oscar, 9
Haraway, Donna, 8
Harding, Sandra, 7
Hartsock, Nancy, 7
Hekman, Susan, 8
Hochschild, Arlie, 93–94, 118

household labor: balancing work and
family (*see* family domain); boredom,
30; childcare, 3, 4, 31, 53, 55, 58, 62,
66, 68, 71, 80, 85, 156, 162; everyday
racism, 139–147, 148, 153, 160; gendered
divisions of work (*see* gender roles);
hosting guests, 101–111; housewives'
strategy to mitigate distress, 100,
107, 122–123; husbands and reverse
traditional roles, 3, 86–88, 158; meaning
of work and housework, 2–3, 57–66;
negotiating, 6, 69–94, 95; professional
women becoming housewives, 2, 5–6,
58, 59, 67, 68; skills, 86, 93, 94, 158; suburban immigrant housewives, 59–63.
See also family domain; *housewifelization*; racial discrimination/inequality;
work domain
housewifelization, 6, 40, 53–57, 67, 116,
155–156, 162
housing/living conditions, 39, 41, 44,
104–105, 124, 158. *See also* in-law
relationships

imagined self. *See* self and Taiwanese
female immigrants
immigration/immigrant: acculturation
process, 11; adaptation processes, 9,
11, 28, 58, 154–155; anti-immigrant
sentiments, 64; difficulty and pain,
9; effect on professional women, 2;
gender and—, 2; gendered—in work-
family context, 5–7, 155–157, 161–162;
as gendered process and experience,
2–5; gendering of—, 41–45, 58, 155–157;
leaving careers and family, 44, 46–49,
66, 67 (*see also* work domain); motives,
41, 177n14; patterns, 4; policy, 67; starting immigrant life, 49–53; Taiwanese,
19–23; through education, 41–45; wom-
en's stories, 7; work–family issue, 5
independence, 47, 64, 68, 76–77, 82–83,
129, 149–150, 154, 179n2
Indian immigrants, 3
Indian/Tamil immigrants, 29–30, 31

About the Author

CHIEN-JUH GU is Associate Professor of Sociology at Western Michigan University. She is the author of *Mental Health among Taiwanese Americans: Gender, Immigration, and Transnational Struggles*.